THE FORGOTTEN

ORCHIDS

· OF ·

ALEXANDRE BRUN

THE FORGOTTEN
ORCHIDS
· OF ·

ALEXANDRE BRUN

Phillip Cribb

≈

GROVE PRESS
New York

A Marshall Edition
The Forgotten Orchids of Alexandre Brun
was conceived, edited and designed by
Marshall Editions
170 Piccadilly
London W1V 9DD

Published by Grove Press
A division of Grove Press, Inc.
841 Broadway
New York, New York 10003-4793

Library of Congress Cataloging-in-Publication Data

Cribb, Phillip
     The forgotten orchids of Alexandre Brun / Phillip Cribb. —1st ed.
         p.   cm
     ISBN 0-8021-1500-4 (acid-free paper)
     1. Orchids—Pictorial works. 2. Orchids in art. 3. Brun, Alexandre.
     4. Botanical illustration. 5. Orchids. I. Title.
     QK495.064C73   1992   91–43132   CIP
     635.9'3415'0222—dc20

Originated by CLG, Verona, Italy
Typeset by MS Filmsetting Limited, Frome, Somerset, UK
Printed and bound in Germany by Mohndruck Graphische
Betriebe GmbH

First American Edition 1992
10 9 8 7 6 5 4 3 2 1

Editor   Gwen Rigby

Designer   Peter Bridgewater

Picture Editor   Zilda Tandy

Editorial Director   Ruth Binney

Production   Barry Baker

                            Janice Storr

                            Nikki Ingram

CONTENTS

≈

ALEXANDRE BRUN
1 8 5 3 - 1 9 3 0
≈ ≈

A century ago, when Alexandre Brun painted these dramatic watercolours, orchid rearing had become an obsessive addiction for European gentlemen-gardeners. Orchidmania, it was called, a mixture of scientific curiosity and gold rush. For, as in the tulipomania of the seventeenth century, specimens changed hands for fortunes.

The fascination derived in part from the orchids' infinite variety. The largest of all plant families (in Brun's time there were thought to be about 6,000 species, less than a third of the number identified today), orchids carried the further curiosity that the grower was frequently surprised by the results of his efforts. Every orchid flower has three sepals and three petals, one of which is distinct. It may be larger or smaller than its fellows, of several colours, spotted, streaked, veined or blotched. It may be lobed, frilled or spiral. To the amazement of the growers, each and every variation turned up in bewildering combinations.

The contrariness of the story for early orchid growers was that while the orchids' response to nurturing in Europe's glasshouses seemed a matter of chance, in the tropical wilderness these were the most promiscuous of plants, cross-breeding with other species, even other genera, to create equally fertile natural hybrids.

This, then, was the charismatic subject that, between 1892 and 1894, Alexandre Brun was commissioned to paint by the Parisian collector Emile Libreck. Alexandre Jean Baptiste Brun was born in Marseilles, France, in November 1853. He studied under Cabanel, Carolus Duran and Machard, moving to Paris as a young man, and achieved some recognition not only for his engravings for newspapers of wartime naval events, but also for his notable maritime works (of which there are two in the Musée de Marine in Paris) and family portraits exhibited at the annual Salon between 1877 and 1934. He also claimed to have assisted in the painting of the mural at the Musée d'Océanographie, Monaco, a task which apparently achieved him an entrée to the opening celebrations in 1920, at the personal invitation of the monarch, Prince Albert I.

In 1886, aged 33, Brun married Lucille Dutheil. When, a few years later, her much younger sister, Louise-Emilie (known as Zellie or Mimie) and brother, Hippolyte, were orphaned, they were placed in the care of their mother's relations, the Libreck family. Emile Libreck carried this guardianship through once his parents died in 1897 and 1907.

Emile Libreck was a wealthy young Parisian for whom it was fashionable to grow orchids. Keen to have his orchids recorded for posterity, particularly having nurtured some superb blooms in the early years of their introduction, he turned to the immediate family of his parents' ward, since he was very well acquainted with the artist Alexandre Brun, who was married to Zellie's older sister, Lucille.

In 1895, to his great pride and pleasure, Emile Libreck's orchid collection was awarded a Bronze Medal by the Société Nationale d'Horticulture de France. It became one of his most prized possessions.

Born in 1879, Zellie would have been in her teens by the time Emile Libreck approached Brun to paint his precious orchids in flower. The idea of hastily written messages and the scurry of activity needed to capture some briefly blooming beauty lends some intrigue to the history of the paintings. Certainly an elderly Zellie recalled how she had loved to watch her brother-in-law paint the orchids, which he did using a dark wash for the background to produce the dramatic paintings we see today.

At some time, once the commission was complete, the paintings were placed in two splendid leather volumes, inscribed with the word Orchidées, *and the belief is that when Libreck died he left the collection and his prize medallion to the artist, his friend Alexandre Brun.*

Brun and Lucille continued to have a lifelong, caring relationship with Zellie, although on her travels abroad she met, and in 1912 married, an English doctor serving with the Indian Medical Service. She joined him in India where their only child, Mary, was born in 1914; shortly after her birth the couple returned to live in England.

Zellie and her husband William—an amateur artist—kept in close contact with Lucille and Alexandre and visited their family. Their correspondence included discussions on art and the sale of Brun's paintings in England. In 1923 Alexandre sent Zellie the collection of orchid paintings, which she tried to annotate and name, but she faltered on the nomenclature of some and, indeed, many of the orchids have now been given new and different names.

When Zellie died in the 1950s, her daughter, also a doctor, inherited her many French, Indian and family mementoes, but the collections regrettably fell into the shadows and were left boxed and stored in various bank vaults and attics.

Some 30 years later, the paintings caught the enthusiasm and imagination of Mary's daughter-in-law, the author of this introduction, who found them, still boxed away but in superb condition. In 1981 the Royal Horticultural Society accepted the paintings for exhibition at their annual orchid show, but the Judging Committee was faced with a dilemma, since it had never awarded a medal to an artist posthumously. Finally a decision was taken to award a Gold Medal to the exhibitor. The orchids had won another medal, nearly 100 years after Libreck had been awarded his splendid bronze medallion in Paris. The paintings were later successfully exhibited in London and in Norwich Castle, Norfolk.

It seems a little ironic that Brun's major maritime works have not achieved the recognition that a private commission, executed for a friend, has finally brought him. He died "a splendid old man", apparently back in his beloved Marseilles, in a house close to the sea.

BRIDGET ROSS

Little is known of Emile Libreck's life—even the date of his death is uncertain. But this photograph reveals him as very much the product of his time and social background.

PAPHIOPEDILUM INSIGNE

(WALLICH EX LINDLEY) PFITZER

 The genus *Paphiopedilum*, with 65 known
species of slipper orchid, was established
in 1886 by the German botanist Ernst
Pfitzer. *Paphiopedilum insigne*, the first tropical
slipper orchid to be introduced into cultivation in
the early 1820s, was described in 1821 by John
Lindley as *Cypripedium insigne*; Pfitzer transferred
it to *Paphiopedilum* in 1889. The orchid had been
sent to England by Nathaniel Wallich, a Danish
physician and botanist who was Superintendent of
the Calcutta Botanic Gardens (1817–46). It has a
limited distribution in the state of Meghalaya in
northeast India, where it grows at 3,300–5,000 ft /
1,000–1,500 m, usually on limestone outcrops near
waterfalls and in light shade.

It is valued in cultivation for its hardiness and for
the handsome, long-lasting flowers it produces from
October to December. It was an important parent in
the early artificial hybridization of slipper orchids,
and its influence can be seen in many modern
hybrids, particularly those with a heavily spotted
upper sepal. Several varieties are recognized.

$\mathscr{P}$APHIOPEDILUM ROTHSCHILDIANUM

(H. G. REICHENBACH) STEIN

....

 Of all the slipper orchids, *Paphiopedilum rothschildianum* is undoubtedly the most spectacular and, possibly, one of the rarest in nature. It has been located in only two sites on the lower slopes of Mount Kinabalu in Borneo, both of which are under threat from logging, mining and shifting cultivation. The species was named in 1888 by H. G. Reichenbach as *Cypripedium rothschildianum*, in honour of the eminent nineteenth-century orchid grower Baron Ferdinand Rothschild. It was transferred to the genus *Paphiopedilum* in 1892 by Berthold Stein, a German botanist.

In the wild this orchid grows on the cliffs of steep ravines, with its roots completely embedded in leafy humus. It usually flowers in April and May, but well-grown plants may flower whenever new growth is completed. It is pollinated by hover flies which lay their eggs on the staminode, attracted by the resemblance of its hairs to an aphid colony—the normal brood site of the larvae. This orchid grows easily from seed, and it has been used to produce some spectacular hybrids.

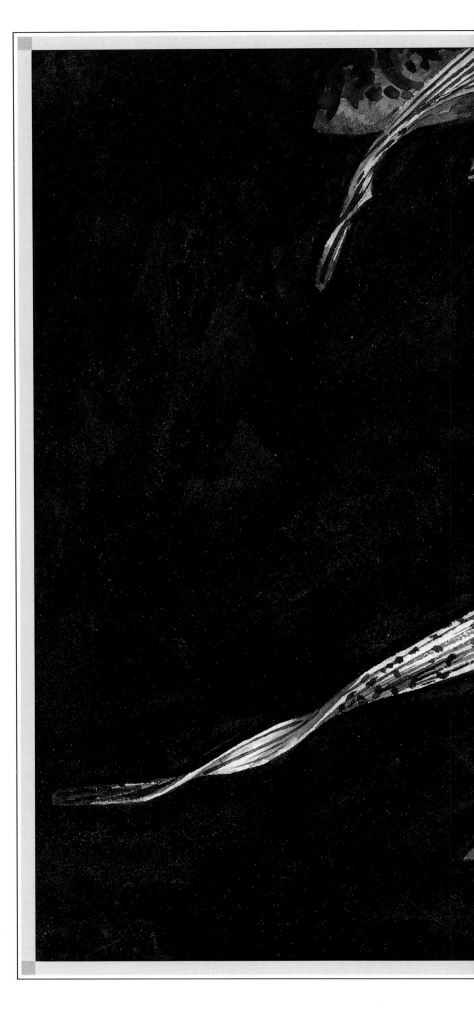

$\mathscr{P}$APHIOPEDILUM SPICERIANUM

(H. G. REICHENBACH EX MASTERS & T. MOORE) PFITZER

....

This charming orchid is characterized by the elegant, large white dorsal sepal, marked with a maroon vein, which arches over the lip. It was sent to Herbert Spicer of Godalming, Surrey, by his son who was a teaplanter in Assam. Spicer flowered it in 1878, then sold his plant to Veitch's nursery for 75 guineas. Masters and Moore, editors of *The Gardeners' Chronicle*, described it as *Cypripedium spicerianum*, the name coined by H. G. Reichenbach; in 1888 Ernst Pfitzer transferred it to the genus *Paphiopedilum*.

P. spicerianum is found in northeast India and adjacent Burma on limestone outcrops at 1,000–4,300 ft / 300–1,300 m, where it is always damp, with mists rising from the nearby rivers. The plants grow in shallow, humus-filled niches, anchored to the rocks by their long roots, with their leaves almost pendent and their flower stalks almost at right angles to the ground. One of the first slipper orchids to be hybridized successfully, its role in the production of modern *Paphiopedilum* hybrids cannot be overestimated.

≈

PAPHIOPEDILUM VICTORIA-REGINA

(SANDER) M. WOOD

....

 In 1892 this beautiful plant was named *Cypripedium victoria-regina*, after Queen Victoria, by Frederick Sander, the outstanding orchid nurseryman of his day. It was not until 1976 that Mark Wood transferred it to the genus *Paphiopedilum*. For almost a century, the species was known under the later name, *P. chamberlainianum*, after Joseph Chamberlain, who became Secretary of State for the Colonies. But since *P. chamberlainianum* has been shown to be conspecific with *P. victoria-regina*, the earlier name is now used.

It was discovered by Wilhelm Micholitz, a German plant collector for Sander, who travelled widely in southeast Asia, Asia and South America. A stately plant, it grows on rocky outcrops in the montane forests of west-central Sumatra at 2,600–6,600 ft/ 800–2,000 m, where there is heavy rainfall and constant high humidity. It flowers from March to June, and exceptional clones have been known to produce up to 32 flowers, although rarely more than one or two are open at the same time.

≈

PAPHIOPEDILUM VILLOSUM VAR. BOXALLII

(H. G. REICHENBACH) PFITZER

....

Paphiopedilum villosum is found in montane forest at 3,600–6,600 ft / 1,100–2,000 m in northeast India, Burma and Thailand. An epiphyte, it grows with its roots among mosses and ferns and flowers in late winter to early spring. Thomas Lobb, Veitch's first collector, found this orchid in 1853 in the mountains near Moulmein in Burma and introduced it into cultivation the same year. In 1854 John Lindley described it as *Cypripedium villosum*—covered with long shaggy hairs—a reference to the purple hairs on the scape. Berthold Stein transferred it to the genus *Paphiopedilum* in 1892.

The variety *boxallii* differs from the typical variety in its boldly spotted dorsal sepal and purple-marked petals. William Boxall, collecting orchids for Hugh Low & Co of Clapton, London, found it in 1877 in the Tongku district of Burma. Reichenbach originally described it as a separate species, but Pfitzer considered it a variety of *P. villosum* and transferred it formally in 1902.

≈

$\mathscr{P}$APHIOPEDILUM HARRISIANUM

....

 This was the first artificial hybrid slipper orchid. The cross was made by John Dominy, head gardener at Veitch's Chelsea nursery, who crossed the Indian species *Paphiopedilum villosum* with the Malayan species *P. barbatum* in 1864. The hybrid seedlings flowered for the first time in 1869. H. G. Reichenbach named the plant for John Harris, a surgeon from Exeter, Devon, who had suggested to Dominy that orchids could be hybridized and who explained to him the mechanisms of their pollination.

P. barbatum is responsible for the red flower colour of the hybrid, while *P. villosum* imparts to its progeny vigour and long-lasting, tall-stemmed flowers with a lacquered texture.

During the years immediately following the description of *P.* Harrisianum, it was re-created by other commercial growers in England and Europe; from these originated many of the early named cultivars. A paler flowered one, named *P.* Dauthierii and now considered a later synonym, is illustrated here.

$\approx$

 PAPHIOPEDILUM LATHAMIANUM

....

 This artificial hybrid was raised by
William Bradbury Latham, Curator of the
Birmingham Botanic Garden, in 1888.
The parent plants were the Indian slipper orchids
P. spicerianum and *P. villosum*. The large, elegantly
contoured white dorsal sepal, with a distinct maroon
line, and the way it arches over in the centre, come
from *P. spicerianum*, while *P. villosum* has increased
the size of the flower and given it a highly
polished texture.

P. Lathamianum has itself been used as a parent in
breeding programmes. A noteworthy offspring is
P. Cardinal Mercier, registered by the Rev. John
Crombleholme of Clayton-le-Moors, Lancaster, in
1921. This plant has a small, rather poorly shaped
flower, but since it is a brilliant red (a feature which
appears to be dominant in its hybrids) and its shape
is recessive, it was regarded as a valuable stud plant
and it is a progenitor of many fine, red-flowered
Paphiopedilum hybrids.

≈

$\mathscr{P}$HRAGMIPEDIUM CAUDATUM

(LINDLEY) ROLFE

....

This unusual slipper orchid is a South American relative of the European and North American cypripediums and of the Asiatic paphiopedilums. *Phragmipedium caudatum* is the largest flowered species in the genus, its most remarkable feature being the great length attained by its two ribbon-like petals. About 3 in / 7.6 cm long when they appear, they lengthen by some 2 in / 5 cm a day for the next seven days.

P. caudatum was discovered in Peru by the Spanish botanists Hipólito Ruiz López and José Pavón in 1778–79. John Lindley formally described it in 1840 from one of their herbarium species and named it *Cypripedium caudatum*. In 1847, William Lobb, collecting for Veitch, sent living material back to England from Peru. *P. caudatum* is now known to occur also in Guatemala, Honduras, Panama, Colombia, Ecuador and Venezuela, where it grows in montane forest at 4,600–8,400 ft / 1,400–2,550 m. Robert Allen Rolfe, the first orchid taxonomist at the Royal Botanic Gardens, Kew, transferred the species to his new genus *Phragmipedium* in 1896.

≈

$\mathscr{P}$HRAGMIPEDIUM CARDINALE

....

One of an amazing 447 named hybrids raised by John Seden, the successor to John Dominy at the Veitch nursery, the handsome *Phragmipedium* Cardinale was described by H. G. Reichenbach in *The Gardeners' Chronicle* in 1882. The parents are *P. schlimii*, a pink-flowered species from Colombia, and the primary hybrid *P.* Sedenii, the first hybrid flowered by Seden and described in his honour by Reichenbach in 1873. Later *P.* Sedenii was remade by other growers, using different forms of the parents (*P. schlimii* and *P. longifolium*), which resulted in several forms of this hybrid—*P.* Leucorhodum, *P.* Porphyreum and *P.* Weidlichianum—now considered synonymous with *P.* Sedenii. All have pink flowers with a deeper pink pouch, although they vary from almost white to strong, vibrant rose. *P. schlimii* imparts full flower shape to its progeny and has been much used in hybridizing. *P.* Cardinale, too, has been widely used as a parent in the synthesis of other hybrids.

≈

PHAIUS TANKERVILLEAE

....

John Fothergill introduced this stately
terrestrial orchid, with erect flowering
stems that can reach 6½ ft / 2 m tall, into
England from China in 1778 and grew it in his
famous botanic garden at Upton, near Stratford.
Some years later, in 1789, it was the first Asiatic
orchid to flower in the Royal Botanic Gardens at
Kew. At that time, Sir Joseph Banks, President of
the Royal Society, named it in the genus *Limodorum*
after Lady Emma Tankerville, whose husband
helped to fund a collecting expedition to Africa.
It was transferred to the genus *Phaius* in 1852
by Carl Blume.

Phaius tankervilleae has a remarkable distribution,
from China and India to the Malay archipelago,
Australia and the Pacific islands. In the tropics it is
found in rain forest and scrub up to 3,000 ft / 900 m,
but in southern areas it is confined to lowland
forest. In nature it has become somewhat rare,
owing to clearance of its habitat and excessive
collecting; however, it is widely cultivated and was
used to produce many of the early *Phaius* hybrids.

≈

$\mathcal{S}$OBRALIA MACRANTHA

LINDLEY

....

The Spaniards Hipólito Ruiz López and José Pavón established the genus *Sobralia*, naming it in honour of Francisco Sobral, a physician and botanist. *Sobralia macrantha* grows from Mexico and Guatemala south to Costa Rica at altitudes up to 10,800 ft / 3,300 m. A terrestrial orchid, it is found among the roots of ferns, in the sandy soil of stream banks, on rocky canyon walls and, rarely, in the forks of trees. It was discovered near Oaxaca in Mexico by Count Karwinski, and described by the English botanist John Lindley, in 1836.

Introduced into cultivation in 1841 by the orchid collector George Ure Skinner, the first plants flowered in the Horticultural Society's garden at Chiswick, London, in May and June the same year. Although each flower lasts only about 12 hours, several bloom in quick succession, and plants can remain in bloom for up to three months. *Sobralia*'s flowers resemble those of the showier South American species of *Cattleya*, but the stems and leaves look more like bamboo. Mature plants often reach $6\frac{1}{2}$ ft / 2 m tall and form clumps $3\frac{1}{2}$ ft / 1 m across.

≈

COELOGYNE CRISTATA

....

This is the type species of the genus and it is perhaps the most beautiful. It was discovered in 1819 near Katmandu in Nepal by Nathaniel Wallich, the Danish botanist and physician who was then Superintendent of the Calcutta Botanic Gardens. John Lindley named it in 1821, calling the genus *Coelogyne* from the Greek *koilos*, meaning hollow, and *gynē*, meaning woman, in reference to the deeply excavated stigma. The specific name refers to the finely divided callus ridges, or "crests" on the lip, which serve to guide pollinating insects to the reproductive parts of the flower. *Coelogyne cristata* was introduced into cultivation in 1837 by John Gibson, a plant collector and gardener working for the Duke of Devonshire. It was first flowered in 1841 by George Barker of Springfield, Birmingham, who had a fine collection. In nature this beautiful species is distributed in the forests of Nepal, Tibet, Bhutan, northern India and possibly Indo-China, where it grows as an epiphyte, or on rocks, at 4,000–6,600 ft / 1,200–2,000 m. The elegant, large white flowers, borne in April and May, are highly prized by florists.

≈

$\mathscr{P}$LEIONE LAGENARIA

LINDLEY

....

 Sometimes called "Nepalese crocuses" or "windowsill orchids", *Pleione* species are hardier than most tropical orchids and will thrive, as the latter name suggests, on a windowsill or in a glasshouse with little added heat. *Pleione lagenaria* was introduced into cultivation by Thomas Lobb, who collected for Veitch & Sons. Describing it in 1851 from Lobb's plant found in the Khasia Hills, John Lindley treated it as a distinct species, although stating that it was received mixed with *P. maculata*. Recent analysis of *P. lagenaria* suggests that in many features it is intermediate between *P. praecox* and *P. maculata*, both of which are common in the Khasia Hills at altitudes of 5,000–8,200 ft / 1,500–2,500 m. Since their flowering periods overlap, it seems likely that *P. lagenaria* is a natural hybrid of these species. It is undoubtedly rare in the wild, and cultivated plants are possibly derived from only one or two introductions.

≈

CATTLEYA ACLANDIAE

LINDLEY

....

 John Lindley described this genus of about 50 species, mostly with flamboyant white, pink or purple flowers, in 1824, and named it in honour of his patron, William Cattley of Barnet, near London. Cattley's collection of tropical orchids formed the nucleus of the Royal Exotic Nursery in Chelsea, which in turn became Veitch & Sons. This handsome species was brought to England by a British naval officer and was flowered in July 1840 by Sir Thomas Acland of Killerton, Devon. A native of the province of Bahia in Brazil, *Cattleya aclandiae* grows on scattered trees in coastal forests up to 1,300 ft / 400 m, where the climate is hot and moderately dry; forest clearance has, however, endangered the species in the wild. Most plants bloom once a year, peaking in May. The species' dwarf habit and unusual coloration make it desirable as a parent in producing miniature hybrids, with flowers of heavy substance, dark colours and interesting spotted patterns, when it is crossed with other cattleyas and allied genera such as *Laelia* and *Epidendrum*.

≈

 CATTLEYA AUREA

LINDEN

....

 This beautiful golden-yellow cattleya has been considered both as a separate species and as a variety of the Costa Rican Dow's cattleya. Prominent yellow "eyes" on the lip of *C. aurea* can, however, generally be used to distinguish it from *C. dowiana*.

The plant was discovered in 1868 by the German Gustav Wallis while collecting plants for the Belgian nurseryman Jean Linden. Wallis collected extensively in South America, traversing the length of the Amazon to its source and exploring many of its tributaries. In 1872 *Cattleya aurea* was again discovered by Butler, a collector for the firm of Backhouse in York. It was named in 1881 by Jean Linden.

Cattleya aurea is restricted to the rain forests of eastern Colombia, where it grows on tall trees along rivers at altitudes up to 4,600 ft / 1,400 m. In the early 1900s, it was fairly common in collections, but this is no longer true, and it deserves to be cultivated again as a conservation measure and for its fine flowers. It blooms in late summer or autumn.

≈

CATTLEYA MENDELII

BACKHOUSE

....

 This attractive species was first imported in 1870 by the English orchid nursery of Low & Co of Clapton, London, and shortly afterward by the Backhouse brothers of York. They named it in honour of orchid enthusiast Samuel Mendel who was one of their customers. The well-known orchid grower John Day of Tottenham, London, flowered it for the first time in cultivation in June 1871.

Its native home is on the eastern slopes of the Andes in Colombia, mainly in the area between Pamplona and Bucaramanga, where it often grows on exposed cliffs and bare rocks. It generally flowers in the summer. The flowers of *C. mendelii* are large, with broad segments, but their softer texture has made them less desirable than other *Cattleya* species for hybridizing. Since the flower colour, particularly the lip patterning, is variable, this orchid is considered by some to be a variety of *C. labiata*, the ruby-lipped cattleya.

≈

ATTLEYA WARNERI

MOORE

....

 In the wild, this orchid is found at 330–650 ft / 100–200 m in the hot, humid areas of Espirito Santo and Minas Gerais in southeastern Brazil. It was first flowered in cultivation by Robert Warner of Broomfield, near Chelmsford, Essex, from plants sent to Low & Co by Binot—Orquidario Binot is still one of the most respected firms in South America. Warner possessed one of the finest orchid collections in England and, by 1865, had more than 600 cattleyas in bloom at once. The species was named in his honour in 1862 by Thomas Moore, Curator of the Chelsea Physic Garden and co-editor of *The Gardeners' Chronicle*. Some authors consider *C. warneri* to be a variety of the Brazilian *C. labiata*, for it has many similar characteristics, but it differs in its somewhat larger, differently coloured flowers. It has a sweet fragrance, like that of rose mixed with lily-of-the-valley.

≈

CATTLEYA MOSSIAE

HOOKER

....

The first plants of this attractive species were imported in September 1836, and one of them was acquired by Mrs John Moss, a wealthy orchid enthusiast of Otterspool, near Liverpool. Her gardener managed to flower the plant, a part of which was sent to Sir William Hooker, along with a sketch by Mrs Moss. Hooker, who later became Director of the Royal Botanic Gardens at Kew, named the orchid in her honour, and it is still known as Mrs Moss's cattleya.

The flowers of *Cattleya mossiae*, the largest in the genus, are very variable, especially in colour, so the species has many named varieties. Some authors even consider it a variety of *C. labiata*.

In nature, this flamboyant orchid occurs in cooler parts of the coastal mountain ranges in Venezuela and in extreme northeastern areas of the Andes, where it grows in forests at 3,000–5,000 ft / 900–1,500 m. Today it is the national flower of Venezuela, where it flowers in spring and is called the *azucenas*, or Easter lily.

≈

ENCYCLIA CITRINA

(LA LLAVE & LEXARZA) DRESSLER

....

The Mexican botanists Pablo de La Llave and Juan Martinez de Lexarza described this species in the genus *Sobralia* in 1825 from a plant collected by La Llave in Mexico. However, most botanists treated it as a species of *Cattleya*, and it was only in 1961 that the eminent American botanist Robert Dressler transferred it to the genus *Encyclia*. The Horticultural Society of London introduced *Encyclia citrina* into England in the 1820s, but it was not until 1838 that it flowered in the Duke of Bedford's collection at Woburn Abbey. This orchid is unusual in having a pendent habit and foliage with a blue-green bloom on it. The sturdy flowers, with a waxy shine and wonderful scent, are produced from March to May. It occurs in mountainous areas at 4,300–6,600 ft / 1,300–2,000 m, in mixed oak and pine forests, where the partly deciduous vegetation allows plenty of light to enter. Despite a long dry season, a cool, damp wind blows and morning mist is common. As these peculiar conditions are hard to mimic, *Encyclia citrina* is difficult to grow in cultivation.

≈

ℰNCYCLIA CORDIGERA

(KUNTH) DRESSLER

....

 This orchid was named in the genus *Cymbidium* in 1815 by the German botanist Carl Kunth, from a plant collected in Venezuela by Baron Friedrich von Humboldt, the pioneering German naturalist, and Aimé Bonpland, his French botanical associate. It was transferred to *Encyclia* by Robert Dressler in 1964. It has, however, been known in cultivation for many years by the incorrect name *Epidendrum atropurpureum*.

Probably the most handsome of the tropical American encyclias, *E. cordigera* is easily recognized by its flowers, characterized by the large mid-lobe of the heart-shaped lip, narrow lateral lobes, the low callus and broad, fleshy sepals and petals. The flowers, borne from February to May, are strongly fragrant in direct sunshine, but the fragrance disappears at once if they are shaded, even by a passing cloud. In nature, *E. cordigera* is found from Mexico and Central America to Colombia and Venezuela, where it grows in rather dry, scrubby oak forests from sea level to 3,000 ft/900 m.

≈

$\mathcal{L}$AELIA PURPURATA

LINDLEY & PAXTON

....

 The genus *Laelia*, established in 1831 by
John Lindley, was probably named in
honour of one of the Vestal Virgins in
ancient Rome. *Laelia purpurata* is a magnificent
orchid, which blooms regularly in May, June or July
with flowers 4–6 in / 10–15 cm across. It is a native of
the southern Brazilian province of Santa
Catarina—whose emblem it is—where it was found
in 1847 by a plant hunter from Verschaffelt's
nursery in Ghent, Belgium. Although promptly
distributed throughout Britain and Europe, it was
not until 1852 that the orchid was described and
named by John Lindley from a plant flowered by the
Backhouse brothers at York.
Rio de Janeiro is the northern limit of this species,
which in the wild grows in subtropical rain forests
up to 325 ft / 100 m altitude. Gently sloping hills
stretch from the beach into the interior and the
region has an oceanic climate with high rainfall.
Several different colour varieties of this splendid
and popular orchid have appeared since its first
discovery, and it is widely used in hybridizing.

≈

$\mathcal{S}$OPHRONITIS COCCINEA

(LINDLEY) H. G. REICHENBACH

....

 The genus *Sophronitis*, established in 1828
by John Lindley, derives its name from the
Greek *sophron*, meaning modest, a
reference to the plant's dwarf habit.
Based on a painting by a Frenchman,
M. E. Descourtilz, who had collected it from the
Serra do Mar in eastern Brazil, Lindley described
this orchid in 1836 as *Cattleya coccinea* on account
of its scarlet flowers, produced from March to
mid-October. H. G. Reichenbach transferred it
to the genus *Sophronitis* in 1864. Soon after
this Lindley confusingly published Descourtilz'
drawing in the *Botanical Register* as *Sophronitis
grandiflora*; but this must be regarded as a
synonym of the earlier name.
In 1837, the botanist and explorer George Gardner
found the plant in temperate forests of the Organ
Mountains near Rio de Janeiro and introduced it
into Britain. It has been used in hybridizing
programmes to produce spectacular red-flowered
progeny and many horticultural varieties—one with
bright yellow flowers—are now recognized.

$\approx$

$\mathscr{M}$ ASDEVALLIA TOVARENSIS

H. G. REICHENBACH

....

Masdevallia was named in 1794 by
Hipólito Ruiz López and José Pavón in
honour of José Masdevall, a contemporary
Spanish physician and botanist. The unusual flowers
have three large sepals, joined at the base, which
taper into long tails. The petals and lip are, in
contrast, so small as to be hardly noticeable.
Jean Linden first collected this species in 1842 near
the German colony of Tovar, in northern Venezuela,
and called it *Masdevallia candida*, on account of
the pure white flowers. The name remained
unpublished and when, a few years later, Moritz
Wagener, a German traveller and botanist, sent
specimens to H. G. Reichenbach, he formally
described it in 1849 as *M. tovarensis*.

During the 1870s and '80s, European dealers
imported tens of thousands of plants of this species,
and it remains common in cultivation. Although
restricted to a small area of cloud forest on the
coastal range of north Venezuela, *M. tovarensis* is
still abundant, and wild plants are sold on the
streets of Caracas in November and December, the
peak of the flowering season.

≈

DENDROBIUM DEVONIANUM

PAXTON

....

 Dendrobium is a widespread genus of more than 1,000 epiphytic species, found in tropical and subtropical Asia, Australia and the Pacific islands.

The striking *Dendrobium devonianum*, readily identified by its fringed lip, was introduced into cultivation by John Gibson, who in 1835 was sent to collect in India and adjacent countries by the Duke of Devonshire, a man of immense wealth and extravagance. The duke's gardens at Chatsworth were world renowned. One of the largest orchid collections of the time was housed there in a vast conservatory, erected under the supervision of his head gardener Joseph Paxton, who later designed the Crystal Palace.

Gibson discovered *D. devonianum* hanging from trees in dense woods about 5,000 ft / 1,500 m up in the Khasia Hills of northeast India. During Gibson's return voyage to England, the plants flowered, and later that year flowered again at Chatsworth, displaying a wealth of blossoms. In 1840, Paxton named the orchid in honour of his employer.

ENDROBIUM LINDLEYI

STEUDEL

....

In 1814, William Roxburgh, the Scottish botanist and physician who was Superintendent of the Calcutta Botanic Gardens (1793–1813) described this plant as *Dendrobium aggregatum*. However, he overlooked the fact that the name had already been used for another species; the correct name for this orchid is, therefore, *D. lindleyi*, coined in 1840 by Ernest von Steudel in honour of John Lindley, Secretary of the Horticultural Society of London and Professor of Botany at University College, London.

D. lindleyi was discovered in northern India by Francis Pierard and later by Nathaniel Wallich and first flowered in cultivation in the Calcutta Botanic Gardens. John Gibson brought it to England, where it flowered at the Horticultural Society's garden in Chiswick, London, in 1834 and at Chatsworth, home of the Duke of Devonshire, in 1838. Its distribution is now known to extend from India across to southern China. It grows as an epiphyte on deciduous trees at 1,600–6,600 ft / 500–2,000 m and blooms from March to May.

≈

$\mathscr{D}$ENDROBIUM NOBILE

LINDLEY

....

This species became known to the West through a Chinese drawing owned by the Horticultural Society. Eventually John Russell Reeves, a well-known plant collector, bought a plant in a Chinese market in Macao and shipped it to Loddiges' nursery in Hackney, London. In 1830, John Lindley based his description on one of their plants. A further specimen was collected in the Khasia Hills by John Gibson. When it flowered at Chatsworth, this plant was given the varietal name *coerulescens*. Indeed, *D. nobile* is extremely variable, which has led to several varieties being described. The early hybrid list is crowded with crosses of *Dendrobium nobile*, the first in 1874 when it was crossed with *D. aureum* to produce *D. Ainsworthii*. Some exciting hybrids, with large rounded flowers resembling small cattleyas, have now been produced, mainly in Japan, and the colour range has been extended to include reds, whites, yellows and many shades in between. This species is widely found in India and southeast Asia, where it grows in full sun at altitudes below 6,600 ft / 2,000 m.

≈

DENDROBIUM THYRSIFLORUM

H. G. REICHENBACH EX ANDRÉ

....

When this striking species was displayed at the Royal Horticultural Society in April 1870, it received the highest award, the First Class Certificate. Certainly, the dense, pendulous racemes of *D. thyrsiflorum*, with its white flowers and contrasting orange lip, are an eye-catching sight, but they last for only about a week. Plants were sent to Low's nursery in London in the 1860s by the Rev. Charles Parish, chaplain to the forces at Moulmein in Burma. Sir Joseph Hooker considered it a variety of the well-known *Dendrobium densiflorum*, and in 1869 named it *D. densiflorum* var. *alboluteum*. But the French nurseryman Edouard François André thought the plants were a distinct species, which he called *D. thyrsiflorum*. In 1875 H. G. Reichenbach formally recognized this name, which is now accepted as correct for the species. *D. thyrsiflorum* is readily distinguished by its white sepals and petals, while those of *D. densiflorum* are golden-yellow. It is native to northeast India, Burma, northern Thailand, Laos, Vietnam and China, and usually grows on deciduous trees above 4,000 ft / 1,200 m altitude.

≈

 Aerides houlletiana

H. G. REICHENBACH

....

 The genus *Aërides* was established by the Portuguese missionary and naturalist Joao Loureiro in 1790. The name derives from the Greek words meaning resembling air—an allusion to the type species' epiphytic habit. *Aërides houlletiana* was first flowered in 1868 by the celebrated Parisian orchid grower M. Lueddemann. When it flowered again in 1872, he sent flowers to the orchidologist H. G. Reichenbach, who described it in honour of M. Houllet, head gardener at the Jardin des Plantes in Paris. This delightful orchid was introduced into England in 1873 by Sir Trevor Lawrence, a keen orchid grower and later President of the Royal Horticultural Society, who had been sent the plants from Cochin China (Cambodia). The species has been in constant cultivation in Europe, though it is not common. *A. houlletiana* is found in the forests of Thailand, Laos, Cambodia and Vietnam, but little is known of it in the wild. In cultivation, it flowers in spring and summer, its sweetly scented flowers carried in a graceful fox-tail spike.

≈

$\mathcal{A}$ERIDES MULTIFLORA

ROXBURGH

....

 This species was first collected by William Roxburgh, the Scottish botanist and physician who was then Superintendent of the Calcutta Botanic Gardens. He described it in 1820, giving it the specific epithet *multiflora* because of its dense, many-flowered inflorescences, or flower clusters. The orchid is sometimes grown under the name *Aërides affine*, given to it in 1833 by John Lindley, who based his description on a plant collected by Nathaniel Wallich in Nepal; but this is a later synonym.

Aërides multiflora is native to Nepal, Sikkim, Assam and as far south as the northern Malay peninsula, where it grows on trees near rivers and dried-up water courses. It flowers from May to July.

≈

PHALAENOPSIS AMABILIS

(LINNAEUS) BLUME

....

Phalaenopsis amabilis is the type species
of the genus, established in 1825 by Carl
Blume, Director of the Leiden Botanic
Gardens in the Netherlands. It is said that,
observing a plant in the wild through field-glasses,
he mistook the flowers for moths, hence the name,
the white moth orchid.

It was first described in 1750 by Georg Rumphius,
who found it on the island of Ambon in the
Moluccas. Two years later Peter Osbeck, a Swedish
pastor, came upon this plant on the neighbouring
island of Ternate and sent the material to Carl
Linnaeus, Professor of Botany and Medicine at
Uppsala, Sweden, the founder of the modern system
of classifying and naming plants. Linneus described
it in 1753 as *Epidendrum amabile.*

The species was first flowered in England in
September 1850 in J. H. Schroeder's collection. It
received a Silver Banksian Medal from the Royal
Horticultural Society at the time, and has remained
popular in cultivation ever since. It has also been
widely used in hybridizing. This fragrant orchid is
native to the Malay archipelago, New Guinea and
Australia, where it grows on trees near the coast and
in rain forests inland.

≈

PHALAENOPSIS VIOLACEA

WITTE

·····································

This orchid was flowered for the first time in cultivation in the Leiden Botanic Gardens in the Netherlands, and was described in 1860 by the Curator, Heinrich Witte, as *Phalaenopsis violacea*. In 1862 H. G. Reichenbach independently described it as a new species, *Stauritis violacea*; however, the earlier name is clearly established as correct by priority.

Two distinct forms of the species are recognized: the Malayan form has flowers completely suffused with pink to wine-red, except for the tips which remain green, while the form found in Borneo and Sumatra has greenish-yellow sepals with a pink base on the inner surface. Recently, beautiful albino and blue-flowered forms have been introduced. The flowers normally open one after the other from June to October.

Phalaenopsis violacea has been widely used in breeding programmes, within the genus and with related species, because of its colour and heavy substance and also because its hybrids are generally good growers.

≈

RHYNCHOSTYLIS GIGANTEA

(LINDLEY) RIDLEY

....

 In 1825 the Dutch botanist Carl Blume named the genus *Rhynchostylis* in reference to the beaked column of the flowers of the type species: *rhynchos* means beak. This species was originally described in 1833 by John Lindley as *Saccolabium giganteum*; later he transferred it to the genus *Vanda* as *V. densiflora*, since he had already given the epithet *gigantea* to another *Vanda* species. Subsequently Henry Nicholas Ridley, Director of the Singapore Botanic Gardens (1888–1911), quite properly transferred it to *Rhynchostylis*, and its specific name reverted to Lindley's original epithet. Ridley achieved fame by introducing rubber cultivation into Malaya.

This beautiful orchid is found throughout southeast Asia, but although jungle-collected plants are widely available in the East, wild populations have been greatly depleted. It is, however, easy to grow and is still common in collections. The variety 'Changdaeng' (Red elephant), with deep red flowers, is worth mentioning because of its scarcity and exceptional beauty.

≈

Ascocentrum ampullaceum

(Roxburgh) Schlechter

....

This handsome dwarf species is the northernmost representative of a small genus of about six species of epiphytic orchids. It was discovered in 1812 by Mathew Richard Smith, one of William Roxburgh's collectors, in the forested foothills of Sylhet in present-day Bangladesh. Described by Roxburgh in 1832 as *Aërides ampullacea*, it was transferred in 1913 by the German botanist Rudolf Schlechter to his new genus *Ascocentrum*.

John Gibson brought plants of the species to England in 1837 from the Khasia Hills and it became widespread in collections from about 1865, when Low & Co began selling plants. In 1868, a specimen of *A. ampullaceum* was awarded a First Class Certificate by the Royal Horticultural Society.

This orchid grows on trees, at 1,000–3,300 ft/ 300–1,000 m in the foothills of mountain chains and in hot, tropical valleys, from Darjeeling in northeast India through Sikkim, Bhutan, Burma and Thailand to China. It is popular in cultivation because of its compact size and attractive rose-carmine flowers.

≈

$\mathcal{V}$ANDA TRICOLOR

LINDLEY

....

 The genus name *Vanda* is derived from a
Sanskrit word for the orchid *Vanda
roxburghii*, a species from Bengal and
India. The genus was established in 1795 by the
eminent orientalist Sir William Jones, a judge of the
Supreme Court in Calcutta.

Thomas Lobb, the first collector sent out by Veitch's
nursery, discovered the remarkable orchid *Vanda
tricolor* in Java in 1846, and the next year it was
described by John Lindley, whose work on tropical
orchids has earned him the accolade of "the father
of orchid taxonomy".

Vanda tricolor is one of the largest species in the
genus, its stems reaching up to $6\frac{1}{2}$ ft / 2 m in height.
It grows on the branches of fairly open-crowned
trees at 2,300–5,300 ft / 700–1,600 m altitude and,
apart from Java, probably occurs in the Lesser
Sunda Islands. There is also a single unconfirmed
report of its existence in northern Australia.

VANDA TRICOLOR VAR. SUAVIS

(LINDLEY) H. G. REICHENBACH

 Vanda is a genus of about 60 species from China, India, southeast Asia, Malaysia, New Guinea, Indonesia, the Philippines and Australia. This variety, the sweet-scented vanda, was introduced into cultivation in England in 1846. John Lindley originally described it in 1848 as a distinct species, *Vanda suavis*, based on a plant collected in Java by Thomas Lobb. In 1861, H. G. Reichenbach reduced it to a variety of *V. tricolor*, and it differs from the typical plant in its scent and in having lighter coloured flowers, which are boldly marked with purple.

Like *Vanda tricolor*, this variety is a popular plant in cultivation and it is particularly noted for its strongly fragrant flowers, which bloom in the winter. It has been widely used in hybridizing projects.

≈

NEOFINETIA FALCATA

(THUNBERG) HU

....

In 1784, Carl Peter Thunberg, a Swedish botanist who succeeded Linnaeus at Uppsala University, described this dainty species as *Orchis falcata*. It was then transferred to the genus *Angraecum*, but with its distinctive flowers it is aberrant in that genus; so in 1925 a Chinese botanist, Hsen-hu Hu, established a new genus for it, *Neofinetia*, named after the French botanist Achille Finet. *Neofinetia falcata*, the Japanese fûran, or wind orchid, is so called because the winds afford the major source of collection. It grows in cool forests on the highest branches of ancient trees, having long since been stripped from more accessible perches because of the price tag on its head; but high winds usually dislodge some plants which can be picked up by collectors.
Orchids are tremendously popular in Japan, where they are a symbol of longevity, and the strange variegated mutations of the fûran that sometimes appear in the wild have long been eagerly sought as status symbols. The flowers, pleasantly fragrant at night, are borne mainly in July.

≈

ANGRAECUM SESQUIPEDALE

THOURAS

This remarkable orchid was first collected in 1822 by the French explorer and botanist Aubert Aubert du Petit-Thouars in Madagascar, where it grows on rocks in full sun in the hot lowlands of the east coast. He gave it the name *sesquipedale*, meaning literally measuring a foot and a half, on account of its long nectary or spur, which can, indeed, reach as much as 14 in/35 cm. The largest flowered of the angraecums and one of the most spectacular, it has been given many fanciful names, "vegetable starfish" and "comet orchid" among them. At night it emits a spicy, sometimes overpowering scent. So striking and fascinating was *sesquipedale* to early botanists that it was one of the first Madagascan orchids to be introduced into Europe, in 1854. Charles Darwin suggested in 1862 that in the wild its pollination must be effected by a nocturnal hawkmoth with a proboscis sufficiently long to reach the nectar in the lower part of the spur. As predicted, *Xanthopan morgani praedicta*, a hawkmoth with a tongue of the requisite length was discovered some 40 years later.

≈

 $\mathcal{P}$ROMENAEA STAPELIOIDES

(L I N K   &   O T T O)   L I N D L E Y

....

 John Lindley established this interesting genus in 1843; the 12 known species are restricted to Brazil. *Promenaea stapelioides* was originally described in 1826 by Heinrich Link, Professor of Botany at Berlin, and Christoph Otto, a botanist and gardener at the Botanic Gardens there, from a plant collected near Rio de Janeiro by H. Beyrich. They placed it in the genus *Cymbidium* but Lindley eventually transferred it to *Promenaea* in 1843. It was introduced into cultivation in Britain by George Gardner, who sent back plants found in the Organ Mountains, inland from Rio, to the Glasgow Botanic Garden, where they flowered in 1830.

The luridly coloured flowers of this little orchid resemble the similarly marked carrion flowers of the genus *Stapelia*, which attract flies; hence its name, *stapelioides*. *Promenaea* species have been used in hybridizing, and *P.* Crawshayana, produced in 1905 by crossing *P. stapelioides* and the yellow-flowered *P. xanthina*, is still often grown in orchid collections.

≈

PROMENAEA XANTHINA

(LINDLEY) LINDLEY

....

 This delightful little orchid, with bright
golden flowers, was first described by John
Lindley in 1839 as *Maxillaria xanthina*.
His description was based on a dried specimen
collected by George Gardner in the Organ
Mountains, near Rio de Janeiro in Brazil. In 1843
Lindley transferred it to the genus *Promenaea*.
It is not clear when the species was first cultivated in
Europe, but it was discovered at the beginning of
the nineteenth century by the French traveller and
naturalist Michel Etienne Descourtilz in the state of
Minas Gerais, Brazil. It may, therefore, have been in
cultivation before Gardner collected it; in any event,
it was certainly well known by the 1860s. Since then
its popularity has waned, although there does now
seem to be renewed interest in the
smaller-flowered orchids.
Promenaea xanthina is a native of Brazil, where it
grows on sheltered trees and rocks in montane forest
in the mountains near the east coast.

≈

 *LYCASTE CRUENTA*

(LINDLEY) LINDLEY

....

 Lycaste was the beautiful daughter of Priam and Hecuba, king and queen of ancient Troy, and *Lycaste cruenta* is one of the showiest and loveliest of the yellow-flowered species in the genus. It was discovered by George Ure Skinner, an English merchant who lived in Guatemala, in 1841, the time when "orchidmania" was taking hold in England, and the New World was being combed for its orchid treasures. Skinner collected for James Bateman, then a student at Oxford, and also sent plants to Sir William Hooker, Director of Kew Gardens, who passed them on to John Lindley. Lindley named the orchid *Maxillaria cruenta*, transferring it to the genus *Lycaste* in 1843. In the wild *L. cruenta* is found in Mexico, Guatemala and El Salvador, where it grows in cool, open oak forest at 3,300–6,600 ft / 1,000–2,000 m. It flowers in the dry season, January and February, producing a dozen flowers with a strong cinnamon scent from each pseudobulb. These are armed with two sharp spines at the apex, left behind when the previous season's leaves drop off at the time of flowering.

≈

ANSELLIA AFRICANA

....

This handsome African species, known as the leopard orchid, is valued for its large yellow flowers, which are heavily spotted with maroon markings. Lindley established the genus in 1844, naming it after John Ansell, a gardener at the Horticultural Society's garden at Chiswick, London, who collected the type species in 1841. Ansell accompanied the first British Niger Expedition to West Africa and discovered this plant growing on the stem of an oil palm, not far from the sea, on the island of Fernando Pó.

Lindley remarked at the time, "it is a noble plant of considerable size, bearing a long gracefully drooping panicle of large flowers." It has since become popular in cultivation and several varieties are now recognized.

Ansellia africana grows as an epiphyte from sea level to 4,600 ft /1,400 m in the deciduous woodlands that cover much of tropical south-central Africa, from Sierra Leone across to Kenya and south to Natal in South Africa.

≈

CUTICARIA STEELII

(H O O K E R) L I N D L E Y

....

 Scuticaria steelii is a small genus. The name, based on the Latin *scutica*, meaning a whip, refers to the long, pendent, smoothly rounded leaves. Indeed, the leaves of *Scuticaria steelii*, the type species of the genus, may reach as much as 5 ft/1.5 m in length.

This interesting orchid was discovered in Guyana by Matthew Steele in 1836, and was first flowered in cultivation by John Moss, who had an outstanding orchid collection at Otterspool, near Liverpool. Moss sent flowers to Sir William Hooker at Kew, who in 1837 named the plant *Maxillaria steelii*, in honour of its collector. In 1843, Lindley transferred it to his new genus *Scuticaria*.

In the wild, *S. steelii* occurs in Guyana, Venezuela and Brazil. In southern Brazil it grows in forests on mountain peaks, while in Venezuela it is found in low-level forests along the sides of streams. Although not widely cultivated these days, *S. steelii* would be a fine addition to any collection.

≈

CATASETUM PILEATUM

H. G. REICHENBACH

....

Most orchids have bisexual flowers, but *Catasetum* is one of relatively few genera that have distinct, and frequently different-looking, male and female flowers on separate stems on the same plant. The female flowers of *C. pileatum*, for example, are helmet shaped, with the lip uppermost, while the males, shown in the painting, are waxy and glossy, with the lip below and almost flat.

Catasetum pileatum was described by H. G. Reichenbach in 1882 from a plant introduced from Venezuela by the Belgian nurseryman Jean Linden. The species quickly became popular and in 1887 a London grower paid 50 guineas for a plant in flower. It is still widely grown for its large, showy blooms produced from June to August, which range in colour from white to lime-green and butter-yellow and are intensely fragrant.

In nature, *C. pileatum* occurs in Trinidad, Brazil, Ecuador, Colombia and Venezuela, where the white form, called "Flor de Nacar" (Mother-of-pearl flower) was once the national flower. Due to its beauty, the orchid has now been almost stripped from the wild.

≈

CIRRHAEA DEPENDENS

(LODDIGES) H. G. REICHENBACH

....

Cirrhaea, a genus of about five species found in tropical South America, was established in 1832 by John Lindley. The name derives from the Latin *cirrus*, a tendril, and refers to the rostellum, which is prolonged in the form of a small tendril.

This species was first described in 1824 as *Cymbidium dependens* by the London nurseryman George Loddiges from a plant he received from Brazil, but it has been known by several names. In 1830 Sir William Hooker described it as *Gongora viridi-purpurea*, based on material flowered by Mrs Arnold Harrison of Aigburgh, near Liverpool. She had received plants from her brother, who had collected them near Rio de Janeiro. Then in 1836, John Lindley described the plant as *Cirrhaea tristis*—sad coloured—from material obtained by Loddiges that flowered in 1835. But both are now considered referable to *Cirrhaea dependens*, the name H. G. Reichenbach gave the plant in 1836. Little is known of the species in the wild even today, but it is thought to be endemic to Brazil.

≈

$\mathcal{S}$TANHOPEA GRAVEOLENS

LINDLEY

....

The genus *Stanhopea*, with about 25 tropical American species, was established in 1829 by John Frost, then Director of the Medico-Botanical Society, and named in honour of the Earl of Stanhope, the Society's president. John Lindley described *Stanhopea graveolens* in 1840, based on a plant purchased from the London nurseryman James Charles Tate, who had "imported it from Peru". This must have been an error, since the showy, rather grotesque, species occurs from Mexico south through Guatemala to Honduras and Belize, growing in mountain forests up to 8,900 ft / 2,700 m altitude.

Stanhopea species are pollinated by bees in what seems a species specific relationship. Male bees are attracted by the powerful, slightly offensive scent of the freshly opened flowers. They land on and scratch at the lip, where they quickly become intoxicated and either crawl or fall out of the flower. In doing so they detach the pollinia, which are transferred to the next flower by the bee, so ensuring cross-fertilization.

≈

$\mathcal{S}$TANHOPEA TIGRINA

BATEMAN

 James Bateman, the English orchidologist, named this species *Stanhopea tigrina*, a reference to the tiger-like markings on the flowers, in 1837. His description was based on a plant collected in 1835 near Jalapa, Mexico, by Hankman, a collector for the orchid nursery of Low & Co in London.

The pendent flowers of *S. tigrina* can measure up to 6 in/15 cm across when fully open, and it is often considered the finest of *Stanhopea* species. The flowers are fascinating in their shape and colour and have a powerful fragrance of chocolate and vanilla.

This orchid is distributed throughout Central America to Colombia and Peru, growing at an altitude of about 8,200 ft/2,500 m, where temperatures remain moderate, despite the tropical location. It flowers in the summer.

Although frequently confused with the similar *S. hernandezii* from Mexico, it can be distinguished by its larger flower and rather different lip.

≈

MILTONIOPSIS VEXILLARIA

(H. G. REICHENBACH) GODEFROY-LEBEUF

 The pansy orchid, *Miltoniopsis vexillaria*, was discovered on the western slopes of the Andes in Colombia by David Bowman, who collected plants for the Horticultural Society's garden in Chiswick, London. H. G. Reichenbach described the species in 1867 as *Odontoglossum vexillaria*, but in 1889 Alexandre Godefroy-Lebeuf, a French orchidologist, transferred it to his new genus *Miltoniopsis*. This differs from the closely related genus *Miltonia* in having single-leaved, rather than two-leaved, pseudobulbs and in features of the flowers.

When the species was introduced into cultivation in England in 1873 by Henry Chesterton, who collected plants for Veitch's nursery, Sir Joseph Hooker described it in the *Botanical Magazine* as "the Queen amongst Orchids".

In nature, this species is found in Peru, Ecuador and Colombia, where it grows in montane forest. It is a variable orchid in the wild, and has been crossed intensively during the past 100 years to produce many spectacular hybrids.

≈

MILTONIOPSIS WARSCEWICZII

(H. G. REICHENBACH) GARAY & DUNSTERVILLE

 This distinctive species was first described in 1852 by H. G. Reichenbach, who placed it in the genus *Odontoglossum*. It was transferred to *Miltoniopsis* in 1976 by Leslie Garay, Curator of the Oakes Ames Orchid Herbarium at Harvard, and Galfrid Dunsterville, an expert on Venezuelan orchids. It was discovered by Josef von Warscewicz, the Polish nobleman employed by the Belgian horticulturalist Van Houtte to collect in Central and South America. He was the first to send shipments directly to German gardens, bringing a new era to horticulture there; in England, orchids he collected were sold for as much as £25 a plant. Warscewicz boasted that this orchid was one of his best discoveries, but the bulbs were very scarce and so soft they always went rotten when brought down to sea level, so it was 23 years before living plants reached the Veitch nursery and flowered in 1875.

Miltoniopsis warscewiczii is native to Colombia, Venezuela, Ecuador and Peru, where it is rare. It is widely cultivated, however, and has been used in hybridizing programmes.

$\mathcal{O}$DONTOGLOSSUM CIRRHOSUM

LINDLEY

....

 The genus *Odontoglossum* contains about
60 South American species. It was
established in 1816 by Aimé Bonpland,
the French botanist, and the Germans Carl Kunth
and Alexander von Humboldt. The name, derived
from the Greek *odonto*, meaning toothed, and
glossa, meaning tongue, refers to the tooth-like
projections of the callus on the lip of most species.
Odontoglossum cirrhosum is one of the prettiest of
the small-growing species. It was discovered near
Mindo, Ecuador, by Francis Hall, a colonel in the
Colombian Army, who sent the dried flower panicle
to Sir William Hooker. He in turn sent it to John
Lindley, who described it as new in 1833. In 1875
living plants reached Europe, and H. G. Reichenbach
devoted an article in *The Gardeners' Chronicle* to
the species, in which he wrote caustically about
Lindley's poor diagnosis and corrected it. It was
later cultivated by Sir Trevor Lawrence at Burford
Lodge, near Dorking in Surrey. In the wild,
O. cirrhosum occurs in Ecuador and Colombia in
cloud forest at 5,300–6,600 ft / 1,600–2,000 m.

≈

ODONTOGLOSSUM CRISPUM

LINDLEY

....

This famous species was discovered in 1842 in the Colombian Andes by a German collector, Karl Theodore Hartweg. John Lindley described it in 1845, but living plants were not available until 20 years later.

In 1863 John Weir for the Horticultural Society, Henry Blunt for Low's nursery in London, and Louis Joseph Schlim, Jean Linden's half-brother, for Linden in Brussels, were sent out to bring *Odontoglossum crispum* back to Europe. As a result, in 1864 this species was described as *O. alexandrae* by the English orchidologist James Bateman from Weir's collection, and as *O. bluntii* from Blunt's collection by H. G. Reichenbach. But within a few years, tens of thousands of plants had arrived in Europe and the enormous variability of form became evident, making it clear that these names were superfluous.

At the height of the popularity of *O. crispum* a single prized clone changed hands for 1,500 guineas. The species is still popular and has been widely used in hybridizing programmes. It flowers in autumn to winter.

≈

ODONTOGLOSSUM NOBILE

H. G. REICHENBACH

....

The parent of many of the best modern *Odontoglossum* hybrids, this remarkable orchid was discovered in 1846 at Zuratá, north of Santander in northern Colombia, by the Belgians Funck and Louis Joseph Schlim, collecting for the Brussels firm of Jean Linden. A dried specimen was sent to H. G. Reichenbach, who described it as new in 1849. The species was described for the second time as *O. pescatorei* in 1851 by Linden, who received living plants. Although this later name has been commonly used for the species, the correct name must be the older one, *O. nobile*.

Odontoglossum nobile is variable, both in the colour of the flowers, which ranges from pure white to yellow, and in the carmine markings on the sepals and petals, which range from sparse spots to strong stippling. As a result, many varieties have been described. The species is native to Venezuela, Colombia, Ecuador and Peru, growing in open cloud forest at around 7,200 ft / 2,200 m. It is now extremely rare in the wild.

≈

ONCIDIUM DASYTYLE

....

In 1800, the genus *Oncidium* was established by the Swedish botanist Olaf Swartz, who was Curator of the Natural History Cabinet of the Swedish Academy of Sciences. The name is derived from the Greek *onkos*, meaning swelling, and refers to the warty callus on the lip of the flower. *Oncidium* is a large genus of more than 750 species confined to the tropical Americas, from Florida and Mexico south to northern Argentina. Many of these are in cultivation, for they have remarkably showy flowers. *Oncidium dasytyle* is an elegant plant native to the Organ Mountains of eastern Brazil, where it grows at about 5,600 ft/1,700 m in cool, humid, mist-swept forests. It was imported in 1872 by Benjamin Samuel Williams of the Paradise Nurseries in London, and Reichenbach described it as new in 1873. The specific epithet is derived from the Greek *dasys*, meaning shaggy, and refers to the basal callus.

≈

ONCIDIUM FORBESII

HOOKER

....

 One of the most handsome members of the genus, *Oncidium forbesii* is prized for its large, full flowers, in which the petals bear a strong resemblance to the lip. It was discovered by George Gardner in 1873 in the Organ Mountains of Brazil and sent to the Duke of Bedford at Woburn Abbey. Here it was grown by the head gardener, James Forbes, who flowered it in October 1838; William Hooker named the species after him in 1839.

The species is native to Brazil, where it grows at 3,300–5,000 ft/1,000–1,500 m in mountainous regions in the Serra da Extrema, the western edge of the Serra de Mantiqueirae, the Organ Mountains and Espirito Santo. It is also found in the Serra do Mar, south to Santa Catarina and north to the Serra da Bocaina in Rio de Janeiro state.

≈

$\mathscr{O}$NCIDIUM VARICOSUM

LINDLEY

This plant is one of the most widely grown and showy of all the oncidiums and is remarkably free flowering. It was described by John Lindley in 1837 from a plant collected in Brazil by Prince Maximilian of Wied-Neuwied, a German botanist and traveller. It has since been used as a parent in many hybrid crosses, and it played a prominent role in producing the outstanding *Oncidium* Golden Shower hybrid registered by the Japanese grower Miura in 1984. The species is found in Brazil, where it grows in sunny spots in subtropical rain forests at 2,000–2,600 ft / 600–800 m; in the state of Goias it is also found growing on trees along the banks of rivers. It blooms in the autumn and winter.

≈

RODRIGUEZIA CANDIDA

BATEMAN

....

Thomas Colley, who was hired to collect orchids for James Bateman, found this beautiful species in Demerara, Guyana. Bateman flowered it in his rich collection at Knypersley Hall, Cheshire, in 1835 and named it *Rodriguezia candida* for its pure white flowers. In 1837 John Lindley established a new genus based on this species, naming it *Burlingtonia* in honour of Blanche Georgiana, Countess of Burlington, and the orchid has been widely grown under the name *B. candida*. However, modern authors consider the genus *Burlingtonia* synonymous with the earlier genus *Rodriguezia*, which was established in 1794 by the Spanish botanists Hipólito Ruiz López and José Pavón. They named it in honour of Don Manuel Rodriguez, a Spanish botanist and apothecary who was their contemporary. *Rodriguezia* is a genus of about 30 species of epiphytes, found in the American tropics from Nicaragua to Peru and Brazil. In the wild, *Rodriguezia candida* grows in forests in Venezuela, Guyana and Brazil.

≈

ROSSIOGLOSSUM GRANDE

(LINDLEY) GARAY & G.C. KENNEDY

....

 The genus *Rossioglossum* was established in 1976 by Leslie Garay, then Curator of the Oakes Ames Orchid Herbarium at Harvard, and George Kennedy, a well-known Californian orchidologist. It is a small genus of about five species of showy orchids closely related to *Odontoglossum*, in which genus they were formerly placed.

Rossioglossum grande was discovered in 1839 in Guatemala by George Ure Skinner and sent to James Bateman, in whose collection it was first flowered.

Bateman claimed it was "amongst the most magnificent ornaments of the orchidaceous flora of Guatemala". In 1840 John Lindley described it as *Ondontoglossum grande*.

Later imported in quantity from Mexico by the Veitch nursery, it soon became widely cultivated and is still popular. It is known as the "clown orchid" because the column in the centre of the flower resembles one. The species is native to Guatemala and Mexico, where it grows in montane forest up to 8,900 ft / 2,700 m; it flowers in spring and autumn.

≈

TRICHOPILIA FRAGRANS

(LINDLEY) H. G. REICHENBACH

 This lovely species was found in Venezuela by Karl Theodore Hartweg, collecting for the Horticultural Society of London. It was described in 1844 by John Lindley as *Pilumna fragrans*, because of its sweetly scented flowers, and subsequently transferred to the genus *Trichopilia* in 1858 by H. G. Reichenbach. Lindley had established this genus in 1836, based on specimens collected in Mexico; the name is derived from the Greek words *trichos*, meaning hair, and *pilos*, meaning cap, and refers to the fringed hood around the anther-cap at the apex of the column.

It is uncertain exactly when *T. fragrans* was first introduced into European gardens, but the earliest mention is of a plant cultivated by Lady Dorothy Nevill at Dangstein in Sussex in 1857. A few years later it was imported in considerable quantities by Low & Co, Linden and the Veitch nursery.

T. fragrans usually flowers in March and April, and again in November, and is popular in cultivation. In the wild it occurs in Colombia, Ecuador, Venezuela, Peru and Bolivia, and in Cuba and Jamaica.

≈

TRICHOPILIA SUAVIS

LINDLEY & PAXTON

....

This attractive orchid was another of the discoveries of the Polish explorer Josef von Warscewicz, from the Cordillera Mountains of Costa Rica. When his collecting days for the Belgian firm of Van Houtte came to an end, Warscewicz became Curator of the Botanic Gardens at Cracow.

In 1850 John Lindley and Joseph Paxton described the species, naming it for its delightful scent. It flowered for the first time in cultivation in 1851, in the celebrated orchid collection of Robert Stayner Holford at Westonbirt, Gloucestershire. Holford was also the founder of the Westonbirt Arboretum—one of the most renowned in Britain.

In the wild, *Trichopilia suavis* occurs in Colombia, Costa Rica and Panama, where the finest forms have been found in mossy woods at 3,300–6,000 ft/ 1,000–1,800 m on the volcano of Chiriqui. Here there is a six-month dry season, with neither rain nor dew, and flowers are produced toward the end of it, in March and April.

≈

 ACALLIS CYANEA

L I N D L E Y

....

The British plant collector Richard Spruce, who travelled extensively in South America in 1849–64, discovered this striking orchid in the upper Amazon region in July 1851. Spruce began life as a schoolmaster, but was encouraged by Sir William Hooker to pursue a botanical career and became one of the most celebrated collectors in South America. His most renowned exploits took him to the Andean slopes in Ecuador to collect *Cinchona* (quinine).

Spruce found *Acacallis cyanea* growing on forest trees near streams at Barra, on the Rio Negro in Brazil. It was described in 1853 by John Lindley from Spruce's specimens and is the type species of the genus. *Cyanea* refers to the bluish-mauve flowers, which are almost true blue in daylight. The plant was eventually introduced into cultivation in 1883, and the first plant flowered in Britain in the collection of Walter Holland of Mossley Hill, Liverpool, in August 1885. In the wild, *A. cyanea* is widely distributed from Colombia and Venezuela to Brazil.

≈

ORCHIDS

IF THE ROSE IS THE symbol of purity and chivalry, then the orchid is for many the epitome of glamour and, for some, decadence and illicit pleasures. Orchids have been the most alluring of all horticultural subjects for more than 150 years, collected like the finest porcelain ·by kings, queens, princes, dukes and those who aspired to such grandeur. Orchids had mysterious origins, arriving in London, Brussels and Paris from the tropics of the Orient, Africa and the Americas to be sold for staggering prices at sales where hundreds gathered to bid for the latest novelty, collected at untold peril by an intrepid explorer in darkest and deepest Burma, Buganda or Brazil.

The biology of orchids also intrigued the public. By the 1850s it was known that they grew on trees in tropical forests and they were widely considered to be parasitic, even carnivorous. Indeed, H. G. Wells cast an orchid as the villain of one of his short stories, which ended with the plant's roots wound around the neck of the orchid grower, sucking his blood. Even today, the idea of parasitic orchids persists.

The illicit aspect of orchids can be traced back over 2,000 years to the time of the ancient Greeks, who gave the family its name. In Greece, all the native orchids are terrestrial and most grow over the winter months to flower in the spring before dying down; they survive the long hot summer as underground, slightly elongate tubers. The old and new tubers together

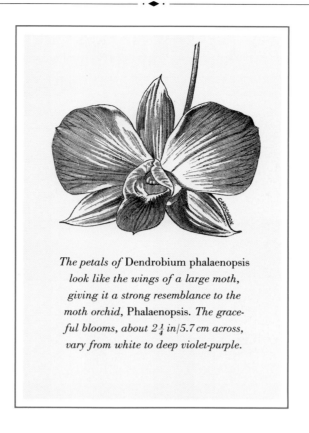

The petals of Dendrobium phalaenopsis *look like the wings of a large moth, giving it a strong resemblance to the moth orchid,* Phalaenopsis. *The graceful blooms, about $2\frac{1}{4}$ in/5.7 cm across, vary from white to deep violet-purple.*

resemble human testicles, for which *orchis* is the Greek word. This resemblance of plant and human organs suggested to the ancients that orchid tubers might be an aphrodisiac. In 1640 the British herbalist John Parkinson, in his *Paradisus in sole terrestris*, wrote that the "ancient Greek herbalist Dioscorides said of Cynosorchis that the root thereof being boyled is eaten as other sorts of bulbes are, and that if men eate the greater, they shall beget men children, and if women eate the lesser they shall bring forth women children: And that the women of Thessalye give the soft root in Goates milk to procure lust, and the dry root to restraine it ...". Even today, in Greece and Turkey, orchid tubers are collected and the ground-up powder from them is sold as "salep" in the markets. In other countries, as far apart as China and South Africa, orchids have found a similar market in native medicine.

It is not only the horticultural and medicinal aspects of orchids that have intrigued and excited man. They are one of the most fascinating, and probably the largest, of all plant families, with at least 15,000 and possibly as many as 30,000 species. This uncertainty reflects to some extent disagreements among botanists as to the definition of a species but even more the fact that orchids are predominantly a tropical group and that the botany of the tropics is still very poorly known. The tropical Americas boast the richest collection of orchids, with Colombia alone having probably

Sketches by the plant hunters were translated into engravings and printed to satisfy the curiosity of enthusiasts, intrigued to glimpse the natural home of their beloved orchids. This view of epiphytes growing in virgin forest in Brazil appeared in De Puydt's book, Les Orchidées, *published in 1890.*

5,000 or more species. The tropics of southeast Asia are almost as rich: both Borneo and New Guinea have an estimated 2,000 or more species. Even in tropical Africa there are more than 1,000 species.

Orchids undoubtedly evolved in the tropics, and no doubt still are evolving, but the family is almost cosmopolitan and orchids are found into the Arctic and as far south as Macquarie Island, near the Australian Antarctic. Orchids occur in nearly every type of habitat. In the tropics they are found on the forest floor in dense shade, on the trunks and branches of the tallest trees and even on the finest twigs of the canopy. Orchids that grow on trees are termed epiphytes, those that grow on the ground terrestrials; many epiphytic

orchids can also grow on rocks, especially in places that experience very heavy rainfall. In drier regions, orchids survive by conserving water in their stems or leaves, like cacti. Indeed, the African orchid *Eulophia petersii* has a habit resembling mother-in-law's tongue (*Sanseveria*) and flourishes on the margins of deserts.

Epiphytic orchids venture into the subtropics, reaching southern Japan and the southeastern United States in the north, and Tasmania and New Zealand in the south. However, most orchids in temperate climates are terrestrials, which survive adverse climatic conditions by producing underground storage organs from the stems or roots.

CLASSIFICATION

THE ORCHID FAMILY is probably the largest in the Flowering Plant Kingdom. Even if a conservative estimate of 15,000 species is accepted, the sheer number is difficult to deal with, and in such a large family it is useful to understand a little of how the family has been classified.

The thousands of orchids fall into about 900 genera which, in turn, have been divided into subtribes, tribes and subfamilies in ascending order. Botanists have attempted to place similar orchids together in groups and to show how they are related. Early classifications usually attempted to group orchids on the basis of one or more shared characteristics, concentrating upon features of the flowers, especially the sexual parts, to provide clues to relationships.

Modern scientific classifications try to reflect the evolutionary relationships of plants and animals, based on the theory expounded by Charles Darwin and Alfred Russel Wallace in 1860. Often the accuracy of such classifications is still debatable because the fossil record of orchids is scarce and even those claimed as such are open to question. So the relationships between orchids depend on clues from living species. Much additional information from the study of the plants' form, their anatomy and cells has, however, recently been added to substantiate the classifications, and today orchids are divided into five subfamilies: Apostasioideae, Cypripedioideae, Spiranthoideae, Orchidoideae and Epidendroideae.

ORCHID NAMES AND NAME CHANGES

Like all plants, apart from any local vernacular names, orchids have Latinized scientific names, the first part of which is the generic name, indicating the particular group of related species. The second part, the specific

Lucien Linden introduced Cattleya gigas *into Europe in around 1872. Collectors were delighted with its huge blooms—7–8 in/18–20 cm wide and 9–10 in/23–25 cm long—of a beautiful rosy pink, with a deep pink lip mottled with bright carmine and two pale yellow eye spots at the throat.*

adjective, identifies the individual species. Generic names derive from a wide variety of sources; some have been named after botanists and gardeners, such as *Cattleya* (after W. Cattley), *Batemannia* (J. Bateman) and *Reichenbachanthus* (H. G. Reichenbach). Other genera have names derived from ancient sources, for example *Cypripedium* (Cyprus was the birthplace of Venus (Aphrodite) in Greek mythology, *pedilon* is the Greek word for sandal, hence "Venus' shoe"). Most, however, point out features of the plant or flowers of the genus, thus *Aërides* (air plant) and *Ascocentrum* (bag-like spur).

This gigantic Cattleya, *7 ft/2.1 m wide and 6 ft/1.8 m high, was found growing in a* Euphorbia *tree in Brazil by one of Sander's men. Its owner, shown with his axe, was persuaded to part with his prize, which was then shipped to Sander's nursery at St Albans.*

The specific epithets follow the same trends. Most are descriptive: *montanus* (on mountains), *coccineus* (scarlet) and so on. Others refer to the locality or country where the plant was collected: *himalaicus* (from the Himalayas), *africanus* (from Africa). Many collectors, gardeners and botanists are also commemorated but the large nineteenth-century nurseries appropriated the more spectacular species, many of the finest bearing the names of Sander, Veitch, Low, Linden and Loddiges. Orchids' names contain information of interest to both botanists and growers. Two species with the same generic name can be assumed to be closely related and to have certain characteristics in common; if it and the specific epithet are descriptive, this may also aid identification.

The discovery of new tropical orchids proceeded in a spasmodic fashion over the years, as distant lands were visited by collectors. This has led to many orchids being described as new to science more than once. The original descriptions are scattered through dozens of journals and books, while the original specimens upon which the botanist based his description—the types—are to be found in many herbaria, where the pressed plant specimens are preserved for reference.

If two names refer to the same species, the earlier name is considered the correct one, a process that has led to many name changes in orchids and to frustration on the part of growers. Multiple names for a single species are most frequent in those with a wide distribution, but names can change for other reasons. As orchids become better known, reclassification may become necessary to reflect that better understanding, and a species may be transferred from the genus in which it was first described to another. Plants may also be misidentified when they are introduced into cultivation and so become well known under the wrong name, which will of necessity be changed when the plant's correct identity is established.

One of the most splendid laelias is the white L. anceps *'Dawsonii'. The convoluted lobes of its lip are stained underneath with purple and streaked with purple inside, while the deeply coloured mid-lobe is rimmed with white.*

THE STRUCTURE OF ORCHIDS

THE DIVERSITY OF form found in the orchid family is amazing. The smallest is probably *Bulbophyllum minutissimum* from Australia, which is no more than a few millimetres tall when in full flower, while the liana-like *Vanilla* species that climb up into the tallest trees may reach 130 ft/40 m or more long. But vanillas are by no means the bulkiest of tropical orchids; some giant specimens of *Grammatophyllum speciosum*, the southeast Asian epiphytic leopard orchid, may weigh a ton or more, indeed a two-ton specimen was exhibited at the Crystal Palace in London, when it opened in 1851. The flowers are equally variable. The orchids of commerce such as odontoglossums, cymbidiums and cattleyas have large showy flowers, often 4 in/10 cm or more across. However, many more species have relatively insignificant flowers, those of many *Stelis* and *Pleurothallis* from the tropical Americas and *Bulbophyllum* and *Phreatia* species from the Old World tropics being only $\frac{1}{10}$ in/2–3 mm across.

Described by its discoverer as "big enough to fill a Pickford's [furniture] van", Grammatophyllum speciosum *bears its golden-brown spotted flowers on 6-ft/1.8-m long spikes.*

THE FLOWER

The distinctive features of orchids, which separate them from other flowering plants, lie primarily in their flowers. Orchids have flowers which are simple in structure and yet highly modified from the more typical monocotyledon flower, such as a tulip or lily, to which they are distantly allied. These characteristically have their floral parts arranged in threes or multiples of three in several whorls, and orchids follow the same pattern. In *Laelia*, for example, which is typical of many of the most popular cultivated orchids, the outer whorl of the flower is the calyx, which consists of three petal-like and attractively coloured sepals. The two lateral sepals differ slightly from the upper one, called the dorsal, or median, sepal. In some orchids, such as dendrobiums and bulbophyllums, the lateral sepals are united to the foot of the column, while in others, notably the slipper orchids, the lateral sepals are united to their apex.

The inner whorl, or corolla, comprises three brightly coloured petals. The two lateral petals are like the dorsal sepal in coloration and shape and differ markedly from the third petal, which lies at the bottom of the flower and is generally striking in its shape, size and structure. This is known as the lip or labellum or, in cypripediums and paphiopedilums, the pouch. It is an important adaptation of the orchid to facilitate cross-pollination and acts rather like a brightly coloured flag to attract potential and specific pollinators. In *Laelia* the lip has three lobes and a two-ridged callus on its upper surface. In other orchids it may be adorned with a callus of raised ridges, lamellae, tufts or areas of hair, or glands. In many species, the

The curious, inverted flowers of Cycnoches
chlorochilon *have the lip at the top; as a result,
the column curves upward, suggesting a swan's
neck and giving the genus its common name.*

lip is extended at the base to form a spur, which can contain nectar; this, too, is important in attracting pollinators.

The central part of the flower shows the greatest modifications, for the male and female organs—the stamens and pistil—which are separate in other flowers, are fused into a single structure called the column. The more primitive the orchid, the less complete the fusion between the stamens and pistil; in slipper orchids, for example, there are two anthers on the column. In most orchids a single anther, the fertile part of the stamen, lies at the apex of the column. This does not contain powdery pollen as in most plants but, depending on the species, two, four or eight distinct pollen masses, known as pollinia, are attached to a sticky mass, the visicidium.

Situated below and behind the anther in *Laelia*, on the ventral surface of the column, is a sticky lobed cavity, the stigma, which with the ovary forms the pistil of the flower. This receives and holds the pollinia, to effect fertilization of the thousands of minute, dustlike seeds contained in the ovary that lies below the flower.

Most orchids have bisexual flowers, with both male and female parts present, but a few have developed distinct male and female flowers. The best known of these are in the tropical American genera *Catasetum* and *Cycnoches*. In the swan orchid, *Cycnoches egertonianum*, for example, the female flowers have a large, fleshy convex lip at the top and the column lacks an anther. The male flower has a small lobed lip at the bottom and has an anther but lacks a functional stigma.

An interesting feature of the development of many orchid flowers is the phenomenon of resupination. Although in the bud the lip is uppermost, in most species it is at the bottom of the open flower, a position it achieves by the twisting of the flower stalk, or ovary, through 180 degrees as the bud develops.

THE INFLORESCENCE

Orchids carry their flowers in a variety of ways, even within the same genus. They are usually borne on

The charming little Paphiopedilum
concolor *bears one creamy-yellow flower, spotted
with maroon, on a 2-in/5-cm stem that rises from
the centre of dark green leaves, mottled with grey
above and purple underneath.*

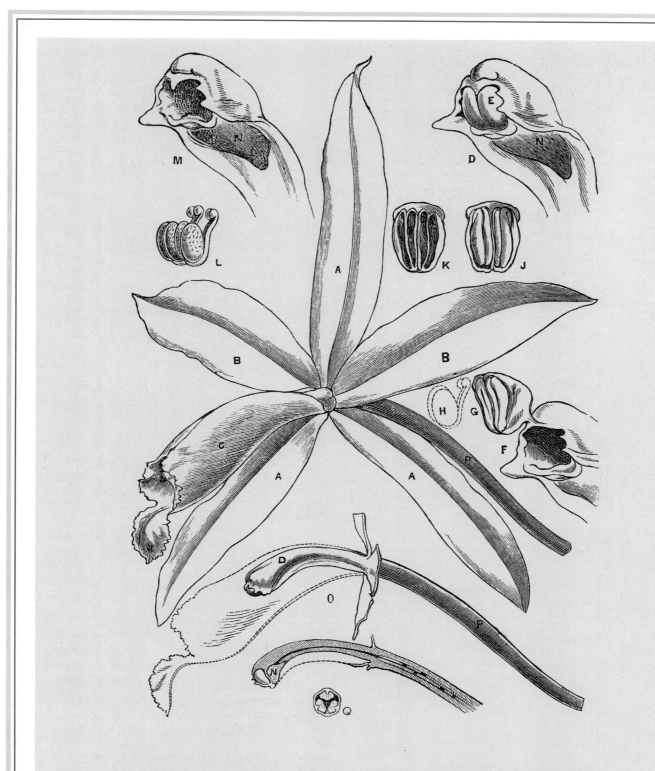

FLOWER OF *LAELIA* TO SHOW ITS VARIOUS PARTS

A   *Sepals*

B   *Petals*

C   *Lip*

D   *(At top) Lip etc. removed to show the column*

E   *Anthers at the top of the column, magnified*

F   *Anther with pollen masses, G, H, uplifted*

J   *Anther detached from the column with pollen masses in situ*

K   *Interior of anther*

L   *Pollen masses removed from the anther, showing discs and caudicles*

M   *Column from which the anther has been removed*

N   *Stigmatic surface*

O   *Lip removed to show D, the column*

P   *Ovary*

Q   *Ovary cut cross-wise to show the three parietal placentas*

scapes—long stalks coming straight from the base of the stem—or spikes, with two or more flowers. Some species produce flowers only when the stem is mature, others when the stem is partially developed and a few from new growth.

In cypripediums the inflorescence, or flowerhead, grows from the middle of the most recent mature growth, but more commonly it arises from the base of an ordinary stem or the joint of a bulblike stem.

In *Cymbidium finlaysonianum* the flowers are borne in a long, pendent unbranched raceme, with the flowers arranged in a lax spiral around the stem; in others such as *Laelia gouldiana*, the raceme is still many-flowered but erect, while in *Cattleya labiata* the inflorescence is reduced to two or three flowers in an erect spike. In several species of *Bulbophyllum* the flowers all face to the same side of the stem, but the most spectacular are those such as *Bulbophyllum mastersianun*, where the flowers appear to come from the top of the stalk in an umbel, and the inflorescence

resembles the head of a daisy. Inflorescences with many flowers are not uncommon in orchids, particularly among the vandoid genera, while in other species the flowers are produced one at a time. Solitary flowers are found in many genera such as *Sophronitis* and *Bulbophyllum* and in some slipper orchids, *Paphiopedilum hookerae*, for example.

VEGETATIVE FEATURES

Orchids grow in almost every situation: from arctic grassland to the permanently moist floor of the lowland tropical rain forest; in the highest branches of tall forest trees, where heavy rainfall is followed by scorching sun for hours on end; on rocks near the summit of tropical mountains; even on roadside verges. The major adaptations seen in orchids' growth and development have evolved to combat adverse environmental conditions, in particular, the problems of water conservation. That tropical orchids might suffer from periodic lack of water is not

This remarkable display of Laelia anceps *var.* grandiflora *was grown on a teakwood raft 45 in/114 cm long and 30 in/75 cm wide. It contained 500–600 pseudobulbs and, in 1886, when this drawing was made, 60 tall spikes, some bearing three or four flowers each, were in full bloom.*

The graceful flower spikes of Encyclia
(Epidendrum) vitellina *'Majus' grow from large
oval pseudobulbs, with the orange-scarlet
flowers borne in clusters around the stem.*

immediately obvious. In many places, even in the tropics, rainfall patterns are markedly seasonal, and most tropical orchids are epiphytic or lithophytic, growing on the trunks, branches and twigs of trees or on rocks, where water runs off rapidly and the orchids dry quickly in the sunshine that follows the rain. In order to survive these periodic droughts, many orchids have developed distinctive adaptations.

In some the stem has developed into a water storage organ; in tropical orchids this is so common that the resulting structure has been given the technical name of a pseudobulb. Even these differ widely. *Cymbidium finlaysonianum*, which is often found growing on rocks, has pseudobulbous stems like large eggs. In *Cymbidium*, *Dendrobium* and *Cattleya* the pseudobulb comprises several nodes, while in *Bulbophyllum* it has only one. Pseudobulbs are also found in many terrestrial orchids and can grow either above the ground as in *Calanthe* or underground as in many *Eulophia* species. A few terrestrial orchids, *Habenaria*

and *Orchis* for example, lack pseudobulbs but have underground tuberoids with which they survive drought. In others, such as the jewel orchids *Macodes* and *Goodyera*, the stems are succulent but not swollen. The horizontal stem, or rhizome, creeps along the ground in the leaf litter, and erect shoots bearing leaves are sent up periodically.

The leaf is another organ that has undergone dramatic modification. Fleshy or leathery leaves, such as those of most *Cattleya*, *Oncidium* or *Cymbidium* species, are common. The leaves of species growing in drier places can be smooth and rounded as in *Scuticaria* and *Papilionanthe*, while in genera such as *Taeniophyllum* and *Chiloschista* the leaves have been reduced to scales, and their role in photosynthesis has been taken over by the often flattened green roots.

A few terrestrial orchids also are leafless, but they lack chlorophyll altogether and are termed *saprophytes*. They can be found in genera as diverse as *Cystorchis*, *Eulophia*, *Gastrodia* and *Galeola*, which

*In the flowering season, plants of the
rare* Oncidium leopoldianum *can be
covered with blooms—white with
purple marks and a purple lip. The
straplike leaves are leathery and the
roots are covered with velamen.*

can form liana-like plants many yards in length. Lacking chlorophyll, the plants cannot photosynthesize and must obtain all of their nutrition from the mycorrhizal fungus with which they are associated. In the case of *Galeola* the fungal associate is said to be the wood-rotting fungus *Armillaria*. Perhaps the most extraordinary of all orchids are the rare underground orchids (*Rhizanthella*) from Australia. Their rhizome is subterranean and the flowers are clustered in a short head that lies just below the surface of the leaf litter, which is pushed aside by bracts surrounding the flowers at flowering time.

Some of the green-leaved terrestrial species of the perpetually moist tropical forest floor have beautifully marked leaves, ranging from green to deep purple or black and silver, with a network of gold or red veins. Not surprisingly, they are popularly known as the jewel orchids.

In most epiphytic orchids the roots, which resemble long bootlaces, have themselves become adapted to attach the plant and to take up water and nutrient in a periodically dry environment. The roots have an active growing tip, but behind this they are covered by an envelope of dead, empty cells called velamen, which protects the inner tissue of the roots and may also help to take up moisture from the atmosphere, acting almost as blotting paper. Even in tropical forest, orchids may have to endure days or weeks without rainfall. In these circumstances, species that have not developed water-storage capabilities in their leaves or stems can drop their leaves and survive on the moisture stored in their roots, protected by their sheath of velamen.

If the seasonal nature of the growth of many orchids is ignored, they will perish rapidly; an appreciation of their vegetative structure will enable growers to provide conditions in which the plants can thrive.

Orchid plant forms are as varied as the flowers. Cattleya aclandiae *has short, rounded, fleshy leaves for water storage, and flamboyant flowers.*

The straplike leaves of Lycaste skinneri, *when they fall, leave a sharp spike on the top of the pseudobulb.*

Bulbophyllum ericssonii, *with its shiny green leaves and slender pseudobulbs, is ornamental even when its flowers are not in bloom.*

THE LIFE HISTORY OF ORCHIDS

ALL ORCHIDS have a complicated life cycle that demonstrates elegantly the interrelationships of living organisms. Successful germination and growth depend upon each orchid's relationship with a particular fungus while, in most instances, successful reproduction depends upon its attracting a specific pollinator, usually an insect.

THE FUNGAL CONNECTION

Our knowledge of the role of fungus in the life cycle of orchids was discovered in the early years of this century by the French scientist, Noel Bernard, and elucidated by the German, Hans Burgeff. Orchids produce seed that is among the smallest of all flowering plants. The seed comprises a seed coat, or testa, which encloses the embryo of 100–200 cells, but there is no endosperm, the food store that comprises the bulk of most other seeds such as peas and beans. The orchid seed has, therefore, no integral food store to enable it to germinate and grow on its own, even if it finds the right environmental conditions. This potentially disastrous state of affairs has been overcome by the development of an intimate symbiosis between the orchid and a fungus called a mycorrhiza.

In appropriate conditions a hypha (fungal thread) of the mycorrhizal fungus will penetrate one end of the orchid embryo through its large suspensor cell. As the fungus enters the embryo's inner cells, the orchid begins to digest the fungal hyphae, releasing nutrients to fuel the growth of the seed. The germinating orchid develops into a small, elongate, top-shaped or spindle-shaped body called a protocorm, which continues to grow until the first seedling leaf and roots are produced. The balance between fungal penetration and digestion is critical until the orchid has produced

green chlorophyll-bearing leaves; at this time the dependency upon the fungal partner declines and may even cease.

In most tropical epiphytic species the role of the mycorrhizal fungus appears to be confined to the early stages of the orchid's development, but there is strong empirical evidence to suggest that in temperate terrestrial species the symbiotic relationship may be important throughout the orchid's life. The European bird's

Orchid lovers were fascinated by the puzzle of how the Madagascan Angraecum sesquipedale, *with its immensely long spur, was pollinated; eventually a moth was discovered that had an equally long proboscis. This drawing shows plants growing on a* Strychnos *tree, whose seeds contain the poison strychnine.*

nest orchid, *Neottia nidus-avis*, and the ghost orchid, *Epipogium aphyllum*, for example, never produce leaves and appear above the ground only to flower. Their entire development depends upon the ability of their mycorrhizae to provide them with nutrients, a testimony to the potential of this bizarre relationship.

A great deal has yet to be discovered about the relationships of orchids and their mycorrhizal fungi. The specificity of the relationship is still debated, and the possibility that the fungi may have a similar relationship with other plants at the same time as with the orchid needs further investigation. The observation that the underground orchid, *Rhizanthella gardneri*, of Western Australia is always associated with *Melaleuca* bushes strongly suggests that this may sometimes be the case.

DECEPTION AND POLLINATION

At the other end of the life cycle, orchids are also dependent upon rather specific relationships for their successful reproduction. Some species produce fanciful flowers that resemble bees, wasps, flies, spiders, monkeys, swans, and even dancing ladies, but a serious purpose lurks behind this charming menagerie. The orchid flowers are designed to attract pollinators which will ensure fertilization and seed production for the continuation of the species.

The earliest study of orchid pollination, *On the Various Contrivances by which British and Foreign Orchids are Fertilised*, conducted by Charles Darwin, was published in 1862. Starting with native orchids, such as the pyramidal orchid and bee orchid, growing on a chalky hillside near his home at Down in Kent, and moving on to tropical orchids sent to him by Sir Joseph Hooker from Kew, Darwin succeeded in

demonstrating the lengths to which the plants will go to ensure pollination and fertilization.

Perhaps the best known of these is the bizarre tale of the bee and spider orchids of the genus *Ophrys*. Many species of these small terrestrial orchids occur around the shores of the Mediterranean Sea and there are four species in the British Isles. Their flowers resemble bees, with the hairy lip modified to look like the body of the bee or wasp and the petals resembling the antennae. The flowers also produce scents that mimic those of the females of particular species of bees and wasps, and males of those species, which emerge before the females, are attracted by these fragrances. This stimulation to the males is reinforced when the bee lands because the lip also feels like the body of the female. The male tries to copulate with the flower and in doing so dislodges the pollen masses, which stick to its body. Pollination occurs when the insect visits another flower and attempts to mate with that as well.

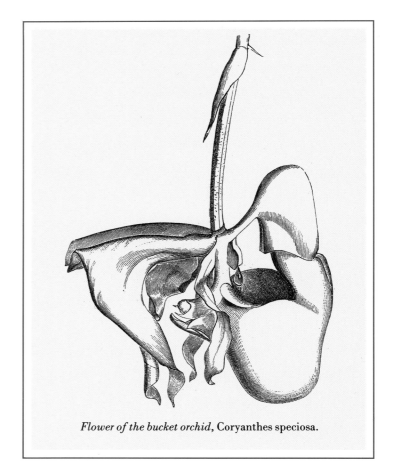

Flower of the bucket orchid, Coryanthes speciosa.

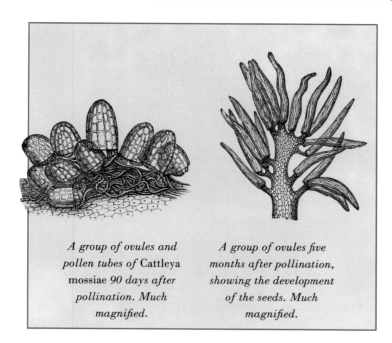

A group of ovules and pollen tubes of Cattleya mossiae *90 days after pollination. Much magnified.*

A group of ovules five months after pollination, showing the development of the seeds. Much magnified.

Indeed, deception, albeit on a lesser scale, is practised by many orchid species to ensure pollination. Many orchids produce little or no nectar but will mimic other flowers that produce copious amounts. Pollinators visit the flower mistaking it for the known food source, and the orchid is pollinated at little expense to itself. The pollination of the spectacular Bornean slipper orchid *Paphiopedilum rothschildianum* by a hover fly also involves mimicry.

The female fly is deceived into thinking that the hairs on the staminode are aphid eggs, which are the normal prey of hover fly larvae. It lays its own eggs among them and will occasionally fall into the pouch-like lip of the orchid. The only escape from this slippery-sided trap is along a ladder of hairs within the lip that passes successively beneath the stamens and stigma. Cross-pollination is ensured when the hover fly visits another flower and repeats its fruitless egg-laying attempt there.

Some of the most unusual pollination behaviour is seen in tropical American orchids. The bucket orchid, *Coryanthes*, is pollinated by bees attracted to the floral glands at the base of the lip, which weep copious amounts of sugary liquid into its bucket-shaped apex.

The bee becomes intoxicated by this rich secretion and falls into the liquid in the bucket, where its wings become wet. It can only escape a watery grave by swimming across the bucket to a small opening beneath the apex of the column, and, in squeezing out, removes the pollen masses. If it visits another flower, the process is repeated, but the pollen masses now brush against the stigma at the apex of the column and pollination occurs.

Pollination mechanisms are usually relatively species-specific although hybridization is not infrequent in some groups of orchid in the wild. Natural hybrids have been recorded in many genera. They are often associated with habitats that have been disturbed in some way, humans being the worst culprits. Some orchids have eliminated the hit-and-miss chanciness of cross-pollination for the short-term safety of

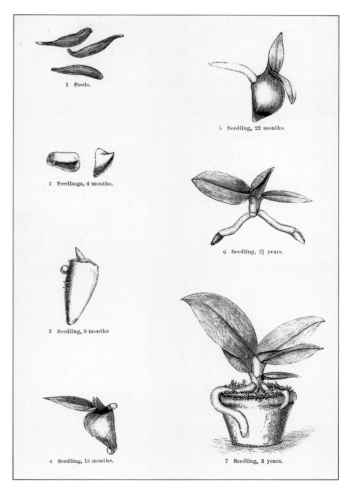

Development of Phalaenopsis *from seed to three-year-old plant.*

*After initial disasters, growers found
that epiphytic orchids flourished in
slattered wooden containers that
allowed their aerial roots to protrude.*

self-pollination. Several widespread species are so successful because they have adopted this strategy, for example, the saprophytic species *Epipogium roseum* is self-pollinating throughout most of its range.

SEED PRODUCTION

Whatever the strategy adopted by orchids, successful pollination and fertilization leads to the production of large numbers of seeds. A single seed pod of most orchids will produce hundreds or even thousands of dustlike seeds. The swan orchid, *Cycnoches chlorochilon*, for example, has been estimated to produce about three and three-quarter million seeds in a single pod. It is perhaps idle to speculate that if all were to germinate successfully orchids would soon overrun the Earth.

THE ECOLOGY OF ORCHIDS

IN TERMS OF numbers of species and the variety of habitats they have colonized orchids are a successful family. They have prospered most abundantly in the epiphytic environment, where there is little competition from other flowering plants. In the tropical Americas, Asia and Africa, as many as 20 species can sometimes be found on the trunk and branches of a single tree. The ground orchids in these regions are seldom as prolific. Epiphytic species decline in numbers outside the tropics and few reach the temperate regions of the world. Indeed, there is not one among Europe's 150 or so species, all of which are ground orchids.

CLIMATIC CONSIDERATIONS

Most orchids have a yearly cycle of active growth, flowering, fruiting and dormancy; even in the tropics few species grow at the same rate throughout the year. In those species with an active growing season and a period of more or less marked dormancy, active growth usually occurs when the weather is moist and warm. In the tropics the growing season is almost always the wet season and flowering is frequently triggered either by the beginning or end of the rains. In more temperate climates, the active phase begins as

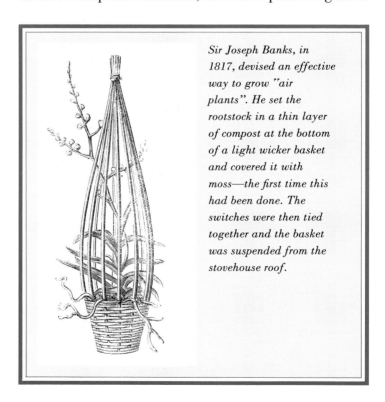

Sir Joseph Banks, in 1817, devised an effective way to grow "air plants". He set the rootstock in a thin layer of compost at the bottom of a light wicker basket and covered it with moss—the first time this had been done. The switches were then tied together and the basket was suspended from the stovehouse roof.

the weather warms up, provided there is also adequate moisture. The dormant period will usually coincide with the colder or drier weather.

Leaf growth and the build-up of storage reserves in the stems, leaves, roots or new tubers is usually completed by the time that dormancy or partial dormancy begins. Flowering often coincides with the end of the growing season, to be followed by seed setting, which completes the cycle. Growers are often surprised to discover that tropical orchids need a rest period, but failure to recognize this has led to the premature death of many choice plants.

SOIL AND SUBSTRATE CONDITIONS

Nearly all orchids have rather narrow substrate preferences in the wild. Terrestrial orchids are particularly sensitive to factors such as the pH, chemistry and structure of the soil. Most tropical orchids grow on trees and are subject to alternating conditions of extreme wet and dry. They cope with this by growing in well-drained places to prevent roots and shoots rotting and by retaining water in their bulbous stems,

Rough bark affords an ideal growing place for Mystacidium filicorne *from tropical Africa.*

thick leaves and tough roots to see them through the dry period. Tropical epiphytes are also rather fussy about their host plant; trees with rough bark are generally preferred. It seems likely that the narrow substrate tolerances of many orchids may reflect the specific needs of their fungal partner rather than those of the orchid itself.

COMPETITION

In the wild, most orchids are relatively intolerant of the competition of other plants, particularly in the early stages of development. Terrestrial orchid plants will survive in a closed turf but will not regenerate readily, if at all, unless bare soil is available. The epiphytic species have chosen, in many ways, an ideal habitat, for few other groups of plants can survive in this comparatively hostile environment. Lack of competition will allow many orchids to grow far more vigorously in pot-culture than in the wild.

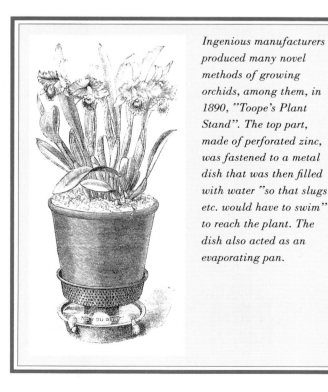

Ingenious manufacturers produced many novel methods of growing orchids, among them, in 1890, "Toope's Plant Stand". The top part, made of perforated zinc, was fastened to a metal dish that was then filled with water "so that slugs etc. would have to swim" to reach the plant. The dish also acted as an evaporating pan.

THE HISTORY OF TROPICAL ORCHIDS

TROPICAL ORCHIDS have been grown in Europe for more than 200 years, at first as a curiosity—but one that rapidly developed into a passion and grew into a mania as the nineteenth century drew to a close. As with so many developments and inventions, the origins of orchid cultivation must, however, be sought in China. We have it on the authority of Confucius (551–497 BC), no less, that orchids were cultivated and esteemed by the Chinese as long as 2,500 years ago. In the *I-ching*, or *Book of Changes*, of which Confucius is thought to be part-author, we find the lines "words by friends with one and the same heart are just as sweet as the aroma of the orchid". The orchids they grew were almost certainly the graceful and sweetly scented terrestrial species of *Cymbidium*, which continue to be grown and prized by the Chinese and Japanese to the present day. Oriental orchid growing had, however, relatively little influence on the origins of the modern tradition that is centred on the cultivation of hybrids of certain tropical epiphytic or lithophytic orchids. This has its basis very firmly in Europe and, in particular, in the British Isles, beginning in the mid-eighteenth century.

The first record of a tropical orchid being grown in the British Isles is that of *Eulophia alta* (as *Limodorum*), sent from the West Indies by Dr William Houston before 1733. The first record of the successful flowering of a tropical orchid in the British Isles is of *Bletia verecunda*, a Bahamian ground orchid introduced in 1732 by Peter Collinson and flowered the

Sir Joseph Banks (1743–1820)

following year. Phillip Miller reported growing *Vanilla planifolia*, from whose pods vanilla essence is produced, in the second edition of his seminal work, a *Dictionary of Gardening* (1768). The first oriental orchids to be seen in the West were *Phaius tankervilleae* (as *P. grandiflora*) and *Cymbidium ensifolium*, brought by John Fothergill from China in 1778. The most significant event of this period was, however, the establishment of a royal connection with orchids which, added to their exotic origins and great beauty, guaranteed their future with the enthusiastic public.

The Royal Botanic Gardens at Kew were established in 1759 by the Princess Augusta, mother of King George III, at the instigation of Lord Bute. At first a modest 9 acres/3.6 ha, the Gardens rapidly grew in size and in the richness of their collections, inspired by Sir Joseph Banks, the Gardens' first unofficial director, and by two remarkable gardeners, William Aiton and his son of the same name, who were successive curators of the Gardens. The elder William Aiton first catalogued the plant collections of the Royal Botanic Gardens in 1794 in his *Hortus Kewensis*. Fifteen tropical orchids, mainly of West Indian origin, are reported in cultivation, brought to Kew by Admiral William Bligh of *Bounty* fame. The first of these to flower, in 1783, was *Encyclia* (then known as *Epidendrum*) *cochleata*.

From these humble beginnings Kew's orchid collection has grown and flourished and now numbers about

15,000 specimens of some 3,500 species. It is probably the oldest surviving collection of tropical orchids in cultivation and some of the plants are well over 100 years old, a remarkable example of longevity of both the plants and the obsession!

Joseph Banks played a further role in the history of orchid growing. At his home at Spring Grove, Isleworth, he and his wife grew tropical orchids and, probably inspired by his experience in Australia on Captain Cook's first voyage of discovery that many tropical orchids grow perched on trees, he grew and flowered his orchids in hanging wickerwork baskets without any soil. Banks's hanging basket was the forerunner of many other exotic containers for growing orchids such as scallop and coconut shells. Of all of these, the most successful has been the open basket made of slats of a rot-resistant wood. Unfortunately, Banks's enlightened attitude, and his success in flowering what were considered to be parasitic plants, almost impossible to keep alive in cultivation for any time, went largely unheeded for another 30 years.

The spasmodic success of early horticulturalists in growing and flowering tropical orchids seems not to have deterred them. Access to plants seems to have been the major limiting factor. The first nursery to specialize in tropical orchids was established by Conrad Loddiges in 1812 and, run by his son George, it flourished for 40 years. Loddiges introduced hundreds of new orchids and their successes are recorded in colour in his *Botanical Cabinet* and in the competing journals the *Botanical Magazine* (founded 1787) and the *Botanical Register* (1815–47).

George Loddiges sent plants to John Lindley (1799–1865), who was then Assistant Secretary of the Horticultural Society of London, to be identified and, if new, named. Lindley first made his mark as the author of *Collectanea Botanica*, a catalogue of the plants grown by William Cattley who remained his patron for many years. Lindley, in turn, dedicated the genus *Cattleya* to him, based on the Brazilian *Cattleya labiata*. A better choice would have been hard to make because *Cattleya* contains some 60 of the most splendid and most beautiful of the tropical American orchids.

Lindley rapidly established himself as the foremost authority on the family and orchids were sent to him from all over the world. He was an influential figure in both the botanical and horticultural communities, in 1830 becoming Secretary of the Royal Horticultural Society and Professor of Botany at University College, University of London. He described more than 100 genera and 3,000 species of orchid and produced a classification of the family which has formed the basis of all further treatments. He also turned his hand to

John Lindley (1799–1865) was the first great orchid taxonomist.

H. G. Reichenbach (1823–89) took over Lindley's role in the latter part of the 19th century.

the vexed question of orchid cultivation because as the hobby of orchid growing gained popularity, so did the death toll of orchids themselves. It was not unfitting that England at the time was referred to as the "graveyard of orchids". Lindley published his contribution on orchid culture in 1830 but, sadly, it scarcely improved matters because he advocated that orchids should be grown in deep shade and high humidity. In reality, many tropical orchids originate in the mountains, where temperatures are moderate and light levels often high.

The salvation of tropical orchids can be fairly ascribed to those few practical growers who heeded the comments of the collectors and travellers who combed the tropics for novel orchids. Foremost amongst these was Joseph Paxton, later knighted for, among other exploits, the design of the Crystal Palace, the main attraction of the Great Exhibition held in London in 1851. In 1833 Paxton joined the Duke of Devonshire as his head gardener and immediately began to experiment with growing conditions for the orchid collection that was the duke's passion. Lindley visited Chatsworth in 1838 and was impressed by the Paxton revolution, publishing his comments on Paxton's enlightened regime in the *Botanical Register* and later in *The Gardeners' Chronicle*.

By 1843 successful cultivation methods for tropical orchids were well established and the first book on the subject, *On the Management of Orchidaceous Plants*, was published by the Irishman J. C. Lyons. His methods were not far removed from those recommended today; for example, the mounting of epiphytic orchids on a piece of wood or other support rather than in a pot full of compost. Another critical development at this period was the introduction, in about 1850, of heating by hot-water pipes by Mr Anthony Bacon, of Aberaman in Glamorganshire and later of Elcot, near

The work done by Joseph Paxton (1803–65) on the Duke of Devonshire's vast conservatory and waterlily house at Chatsworth inspired his famous design for the iron and glass Crystal Palace to house the Great Exhibition of 1851.

Newbury. The scene was now well set for the transformation of what was a hobby for a few to the passion of many collectors.

In many ways 1837 was a critical year and it can be considered the start of "orchidmania", which swept the country and took tropical orchid growing to continental Europe and to the United States by the end of the century. In that year tropical orchids flooded into the British Isles from all over the world, and it is estimated that more than 300 species were seen for the first time. Hugh Cuming sent back the first moth orchid (*Phalaenopsis*) to Europe from the Philippines; the Schomburgk brothers collected orchids in Guyana; Deschamps sent a large consignment of orchids from Mexico; and from Guatemala George Ure Skinner sent the first *Odontoglossum* to be seen in England.

From 1840 onward, the larger nurseries, such as Veitch and Sons of Exeter and Chelsea; Low & Co of Clapton, London; Linden of Brussels and van Houtte of Ghent, Belgium, had collectors scouring the tropics for novelties. Veitch was the first to respond to the growing fascination for orchids, sending out William and Thomas Lobb to Brazil and the Far East respectively. Low & Co soon followed with Low's son, Hugh, who reached Borneo in 1845 and remained there on and off for some 30 years, mostly acting as Colonial Treasurer for Rajah Brooke. In 1851 he became the first person to climb Mount Kinabalu, the home of some 700 orchid species, including the legendary *Paphiopedilum rothschildianum* and the enormous pitcher plant *Nepenthes rajah*, which he named after his employer.

Jean Linden (1817–98) deserves particular mention because of his influence on orchid growing in continental Europe. Linden was a brilliant scholar at the University of Brussels who, at the age of 19, was entrusted by the Belgian government with leading an expedition to Brazil. By 1840 he had travelled widely in Brazil, Mexico, Guatemala, Venezuela, Colombia,

Masdevallia harryana is immediately recognizable by its huge lateral sepals and slender, strangely elongated upper sepal.

Cuba and the United States. In 1841 he was hired by a consortium of English orchid growers to collect orchids in Venezuela and Colombia. His success was ensured when, in Colombia, he met up with Theodore Hartweg, a collector sent out by the Horticultural Society, and together they discovered *Odontoglossum crispum*, that most beautiful and prized of all orchids. Linden returned shortly afterward and set up his own nursery in Ghent, which soon moved to Brussels as L'Horticulture Internationale.

Josef Warscewicz (1812–66), perhaps the most famous of all the orchid collectors, was sent in 1844 by van Houtte to Guatemala, before eventually moving on to Costa Rica and Colombia. He sent thousands of orchids to Ghent over the following nine years and H. G. Reichenbach (1823–89), a German botanist who succeeded Lindley as the leading orchid taxonomist, described more than 300 as new to science. Among Warscewicz's spectacular discoveries, a number of which were named after him, were the flamboyant pink and purple-flowered Colombian *Cattleya warscewiczii* and the gold and purple-flowered Costa Rican *C. dowiana*. The genus *Warscewiczella*, too, was named in his honour.

The major nurserymen received the greatest number of novelties and selected the best to carry their names, for they were not slow to realize the potential marketing value of having species named after them as the flood of new orchids reached Europe. The scarlet *Masdevallia veitchiana* from Peru, and its close relative the purple-flowered *M. harryana* from Colombia, commemorate Sir Harry Veitch and the Veitch nursery; *Cymbidium lowianum* from Burma and *Paphiopedilum lowianum* from southeast Asia honour Low; *Odontoglossum lindenii* from Colombia and *Phalaenopsis lindenii* from the Philippines, Linden. Nor were their good customers, the affluent

The opulent frilled and blotched blooms of Odontoglossum crispum *were much prized by orchid lovers.*

private collectors, ignored, if not all were as fortunate as Cattley. *Anguloa clowesii* and *A. ruckeri* were both Linden collections commemorating his sponsors; the tropical American genus *Batemannia* recognizes the contribution of James Bateman to orchid science and horticulture; Henry Cavendish, Duke of Devonshire, is remembered by the Indian *Dendrobium devonianum* and Caribbean *Oncidium cavendishianum*; while *Paphiopedilum dayanum* and *Cymbidium dayanum* honour John Day of Tottenham, a remarkable amateur grower with a fine collection and high artistic skill.

The possibility of obtaining an orchid new to science and having it named in one's honour must have been a powerful influence on the growers vying for the best in each new shipment, and they were prepared to buy plants before their flowers had been seen. In 1851 the first auction of orchid plants was held in Stevens' London sales rooms; it comprised 200 lots of South American orchids collected by Warscewicz, 194 lots collected by Linden, and 232 lots sent from India. The prices ranged from 10 shillings to £9 a plant. By the 1890s plants were commonly sold for 100

guineas or more, while a price of 1,500 guineas was paid for *Odontoglossum crispum* 'Fred Sander', one of the Sander nursery's choicest plants.

Technical aspects of orchid cultivation continued to improve in the second half of the nineteenth century. The most significant contribution in spreading knowledge of good growing methods was that of Benjamin Samuel Williams, who in 1851 began writing a series, "Orchids for the millions", in *The Gardeners' Chronicle*, which Lindley then edited. These articles formed the basis of his popular book, *The Orchid Grower's Manual*, whose 7th edition, published in 1894, is still the bible of orchid growers.

Two further developments in the mid-1800s were to have an immense influence on orchid growing, but they only became apparent much later. A single pod from an orchid can contain many thousands of seeds and potentially many thousands of plants. John Lindley had reported in 1822 the raising of the South American terrestrial orchid *Prescottia plantaginea* from seed at the Horticultural Society's garden at Chiswick, London. However, little interest was shown by growers until David Moore, Curator of the Royal Botanic Garden at Glasnevin in Ireland, reported raising seedlings of *Epidendrum crassifolium, E. elongatum, Cattleya forbesii* and *Thunia alba*, and the potential for raising large quantities of orchids was at last appreciated.

The second development was the work of the Veitch nursery. John Dominy, their head grower at Exeter, made his first attempts at hybridizing orchid species in 1853, at the suggestion of John Harris, a local surgeon. In 1856 the first of his hybrids *Calanthe* Dominyi (*Calanthe masuca* × *C. furcata*) flowered and was described in *The Gardeners' Chronicle* by John Lindley. Lindley, realizing the implications, commented "you will drive botanists mad", but he

The Gardeners' Chronicle, its title garlanded with orchids, began printing articles on their culture in 1851. In France, Godefroy-Lebeuf established L'Orchidophile in 1881; it lasted until 1893, the year the still surviving Orchid Review was founded in Britain. Lucien Linden's Journal des orchidées (1890) lasted only seven years.

could also have added that it was the horticulturalists' dream: to create their own novel forms of orchid.

The Veitch nursery, which moved to King's Road, Chelsea, in 1864, monopolized orchid hybridizing for more than 20 years before other growers and nurseries caught up. A corollary that surprised growers was the apparent promiscuity of orchids. Not only could closely related species be hybridized, but success was also obtained with crosses between species of different genera. Indeed some of the most spectacular hybrids were such mongrels. It is scarcely surprising that all the major nurseries and many amateur growers in the British Isles were flowering their own hybrids by the 1890s. In France, M. Bleu was the first to flower a hybrid, but he was quickly followed by Bauer, Page, Darblay, Block and Godefroy-Lebeuf; while Linden, Vuylsteke and Vervaet were also active in Belgium.

The dominant figure of the late nineteenth-century orchid scene was Frederick Sander (1847–1920). A relative late-comer in the orchid business, Sander caught up quickly and his nurseries at St Albans and Bruges soon outshone all others. He was born at Bremen in Germany but emigrated to England in 1865. In 1876 he took over a seed business at St Albans, Hertfordshire, and was soon active in the importation of orchids on a massive scale. His first collector, William Arnold, was sent in 1880 to Guyana and Venezuela to collect the pretty white-flowered *Masdevallia tovarensis*, whose recent introduction

had caused a sensation. Arnold's first shipment of 2,000 plants was sent to Stevens for auction but froze there overnight and was lost. This elicited the first of many orders to "Return and re-collect" from the irascible Sander.

In the same year, Carl Roebelin was sent to Mindanao in the Philippines and discovered, in October 1881, *Euanthe (Vanda) sanderiana*, which many consider to be the finest Asiatic orchid. The first plants auctioned in London fetched up to 200 guineas each, but sadly for Sander he was beaten to the auction rooms by Low. Roebelin suffered further misfortune

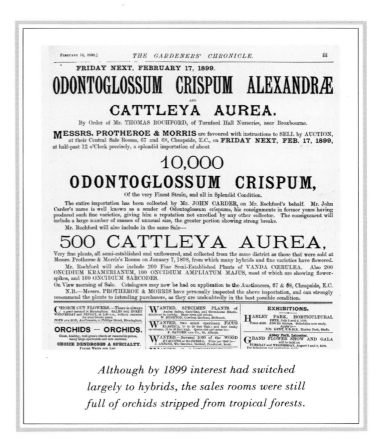

Although by 1899 interest had switched largely to hybrids, the sales rooms were still full of orchids stripped from tropical forests.

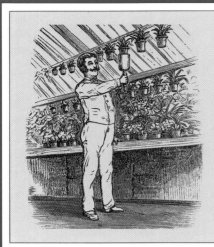

The vast extent of the cattleya house at Veitch's nursery conveys the scale of commercial orchid growing in the late 1800s. More modest growers were advised by Lucien Linden in Les Orchidées exotiques *to water their plants with this device, made of iron or zinc, applying it to their plants "like a lamplighter holds his torch".*

following his discovery of the rose-pink *Phalaenopsis sanderiana*. He collected 21,000 plants, but these all perished when the ship on which they had been loaded for shipment to London sank in the harbour at Manila in a typhoon.

In 1882, Sander employed a remarkable collector, Wilhelm Micholitz (1854–1932), who stayed in his employ until the outbreak of World War I. Micholitz went first to the Philippines to take over from the unreliable Roebelin, but later criss-crossed southeast Asia, the then Indo-China, Australia, New Guinea and the Solomon Islands in search of novelties. Micholitz's most celebrated journey took him to New Guinea to collect the elegant white-flowered *Dendrobium phalaenopsis* var. *schroederianum*. On almost the last day of his trip he at last stumbled across the orchid growing among human bones on a burial site just outside a village. But the large numbers he collected failed to reach England as the ship carrying them foundered off Macassar in the Celebes (Sulawesi).

Sander, characteristically, cabled Micholitz to "Return. Re-collect", but Micholitz wired back that he valued his head too much to revisit the cannibals of New Guinea. He did, however, return in June 1891 and the plants caused a sensation in the sales room in London on 10 October, when one was exhibited still attached to the skull on which it had been found.

Forstermann was Sander's other star collector. In 1884 he rediscovered *Paphiopedilum spicerianum* in Bhutan and brought 40,000 plants back to Britain. The following year saw him in Borneo, collecting two of the most prized of all slipper orchids, *Paphiopedilum stonei* var. *platytaenium* and *Paphiopedilum sanderianum*, with its long, ribbon-like petals almost $3\frac{1}{4}$ ft/1 m in length. The former is certainly lost to cultivation, but *P. sanderianum* was rediscovered as recently as 1978 and once again graces orchid collections.

Sander's flair for publicity kept orchids in the limelight throughout his career and undoubtedly fuelled the orchidmania, that swept the British Isles in the last 20 years of the century. In 1886 he received a Royal Warrant and the magazine *Punch* dubbed him "the Orchid King". The following year, Queen Victoria's Golden Jubilee enabled Sander to return the compliment by preparing an enormous bouquet, more than $6\frac{1}{2}$ ft/2 m tall, of his finest orchids for the Queen. Sander was able to present it to her in person on 21 June. He also commemorated her in the first volume of his monumental *Reichenbachia* (1888–94), a four-volume set of 192 plates touted as the finest illustrated orchid publication. The orchids that adorn it came from Sander nurseries, Reichenbach wrote the text and Henry Moon, Sander's son-in-law, provided the illustrations.

Sander's nursery at St Albans had 12 large glasshouses, each 180 ft/55 m long, and an exhibition house almost 300 ft/91 m long. However, this was insignificant compared to the nursery he set up in 1894 at Bruges in Belgium; here he built 240 glasshouses and grew orchids on a scale never seen before. Sander was, by now, selling plants as far afield as Russia and the United States, and even to the Pope. To supply his growing organization he had collectors scouring the tropics for new species or attempting to find new colonies of particularly desirable species.

The orchid collectors were mostly intrepid, resourceful and often unscrupulous men. They travelled to some of the least-known parts of the tropics, often under extreme difficulties. Such remote areas were explored that they have never been revisited, and some of the exotic species they sent back have never been found again. Competition was fierce and collectors often deliberately misled the opposition or, in a few instances, actually attacked them. Sander complained bitterly that his collectors suffered unfairly from his rival's men. A favourite trick is reported to have been to urinate into the boxes of a competitor's shipment of plants so that they would sprout on the voyage home and be rotten and useless on arrival. A few of the less fortunate or less experienced collectors died in the course of their work. Sander alone lost eight of his men.

The orchids themselves suffered from the rapacity of the collectors. Consignments of thousands of plants of a single species were commonplace, and the death rate during voyages back to Europe was always high. B. S. Williams, the author of *The Orchid Grower's Manual*, complained in *The Gardeners' Chronicle* that "collectors in all quarters are ransacking the forests to send home plants". Herr Ortieges of Zurich likewise complains of the plunder of the tropical forests for orchids. This was well illustrated by William Bull's announcement for sale on 4 May 1878 of "the largest consignment of orchids. The number is estimated at 2,000,000." Such exploitation could not be sustained, and sales in the London auction houses of Stevens, and Protheroe & Morris began to peter out as the century drew to a close. Orchid growers turned to the novelty of hybrids and slowly away from the species that had thrilled them for the previous 60 or more years.

Well before the cataclysm of World War I, the British and European orchidmania had washed away and one of the most thrilling eras in horticulture and botany was at an end.

Sander's ostentatious tribute to Queen Victoria on her Silver Jubilee was graciously received by the queen, but The Gardeners' Chronicle *remarked critically, "we hope we may never look on the like again".*

ORCHIDS IN ART

AS WITH ORCHID CULTIVATION, we must look to the Chinese for the earliest representations of orchids. They were a favourite subject of Chinese painting as early as the Yuan dynasty (1279–1368), with the species of *Cymbidium* the preferred flowers. Another early illustration of an orchid is that in the Aztec herbal called the "Badianus" manuscript (1552), now in the Vatican Museum. The orchid depicted is *Vanilla*, the essence of which was used by the Aztecs, who called it *tliloxchitl*, as a lotion for bestowing bodily strength on warriors, and as a flavouring for cocoa, which Bernal Diaz, one of Cortes' conquistadors, saw Montezuma, the Aztec king, drinking in 1519.

RENAISSANCE HERBALS

The earliest representations of orchids in European literature can be found in Latin herbals of Otto Brunfels (1530), Leonhard Fuchs (1542) and Rembertus Dodonaeus (1583). These contain line illustrations of several European orchids, accurate enough in most instances to allow identification of the species. These herbals were essentially guides for doctors to plants with medicinal properties. Dodonaeus's illustration of the lady's slipper orchid was reproduced by John Gerard (1597) in the first herbal written in English. A little later, William Shakespeare mentions "long purples" (*Orchis mascula*) in Queen Gertrude's account of Ophelia's death in *Hamlet*:

> *There with fantastic garlands did she come,*
> *Of crow-flowers, nettles, daisies, and*
> > *long purples,*
> *That liberal shepherds give a grosser name,*
> *But our cold maids do dead men's fingers*
> > *call them.*

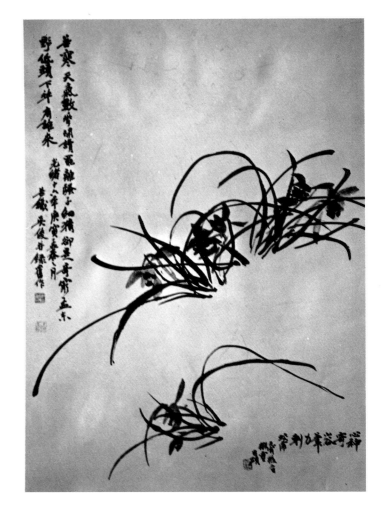

Cymbidium goeringii, *a prized orchid in China since the days of Confucius, is shown in this Ming dynasty painting.*

The renewal of interest in plants and plant properties inspired by the Renaissance eventually led, by the time of Carl Linnaeus (1707–78), to the separation of the science of botany from that of medicine.

LINNAEUS'S REVOLUTION

Linnaeus can be considered the father of modern botany. *Species Plantarum* (1753), his catalogue of the plants of the world, is considered the starting point of plant nomenclature. He also inspired his students to travel and discover plants. The tropics and southern hemisphere were scarcely explored at the time, but during the next century exotic plants flowed into Europe from all over the globe. Since identification depended on a thorough understanding of the structure of the flower, increasing numbers of drawings of plants were published to assist identification. Indeed, the novelties were often beautiful and spectacular plants which inspired botanical artists such as Redouté and Ehret to paint them.

THE NINETEENTH CENTURY

The most accomplished botanical illustrators of the early nineteenth century were undoubtedly the Austrian brothers, Franz and Ferdinand Bauer. The former worked at Kew in the time of Banks and William Aiton, while the latter accompanied the botanist Robert Brown on Matthew Flinders' circumnavigation of Australia. Franz Bauer's work can be seen at its finest in Sibthorp's *Flora Graeca*, but he also illustrated many exotic orchids in his and Lindley's *Illustrations of Orchidaceous Plants* (1830–38). Ferdinand's illustrations of Australian plants at the Natural History Museum in London include many exquisite watercolours of the terrestrial orchids of that continent.

At this time botanical illustrators of varying talents were employed by several botanical magazines whose aim was to introduce new garden-worthy plants to the public. The first of these was William Curtis's *Botanical Magazine* founded in 1787, which today flourishes as the *Kew Magazine*. More than 1,200 species of orchid have been illustrated in it, many for the first time. The best known of its artists was Walter Hood Fitch, who was based at Kew and served it for 40 years.

The main rival of the *Botanical Magazine*, for 33 years from 1815, was Edwards' *Botanical Register*, which for most of its existence was edited by John Lindley. Lindley employed as an artist Miss Drake,

about whom little is known, but of the more than 440 orchids illustrated in this magazine most were her work. Her beautifully executed watercolours also adorned Lindley's *Sertum Orchidacearum* (1838) and she contributed, with Augusta Withers the Royal flower painter, the fine watercolours for James Bateman's monumental *Orchidaceae of Mexico and Guatemala* (1837–43).

The *Botanical Magazine* and *Botanical Register* were only two of many such publications in the first half of the nineteenth century but most of them succumbed to the competition of John Lindley's *Gardeners' Chronicle*, which he founded in 1847. Issued weekly, it allowed the rapid publication of botanical and horticultural articles, including those

A readily identifiable drawing of the lizard orchid appeared in 1581 in the Herbal *of the Flemish botanist Matthias de Lobel, after whom the lobelia was named. It shows the resemblance of the tubers to human testicles that gave the orchid its name.*

July 4th 1884

John Day's painting of the brilliant lime-green Coelogyne pandurata, *a native of Borneo (where it is known as the black orchid on account of its sooty lip) was "drawn at Messrs. Veitch and Sons from a very fine plant." Day comments that although it had "2 spikes of 10 flowers each—I have drawn only 8 [7, in fact] as there was not room enough for any more." Day liked the orchid because it was "so peculiar", and notes, "It is almost the only thing I have ever used lampblack for."*

on new species. Many of the new orchids described in this journal over the following 60 or so years were illustrated by black and white engravings.

ILLUSTRATED ORCHID BOOKS

The nineteenth century produced some magnificent illustrated books on orchids, some of many volumes. The large orchid nurseries used the public demand for finely illustrated works to produce volumes that were, in effect, glorified catalogues of their wares. Linden's Belgian nursery published *Lindenia*; Warner and B. S. Williams produced the *Orchid Album*; and Cogniaux and Goossens the *Dictionnaire iconographique des Orchidées*.

Frederick Sander was not, however, a man to let others steal a march and he determined to outdo them all. In 1885 Henry Moon, a well-known flower

There were several fine lady botanical artists in the 1800s, among them Miss Drake. Her painting of Bollea (Huntleya) violacea *in Lindley's* Sertum Orchidacearum *perfectly captures the soft violet and brown coloration and velvety texture of the orchid.*

artist and later Sander's son-in-law, was employed to paint Sander's choicest plants for *Reichenbachia* (1888–94). This work comprised four volumes in two series, 192 paintings in all. The weight of each volume was 44 lb/20 kg and it measured around $29\frac{1}{2} \times 23\frac{1}{2}$ in/75 × 60 cm. In keeping with Sander's

style, the volumes were dedicated to Queen Victoria, the German Empress Augusta Victoria, the Empress Maria Fedorova of Russia, and Queen Henriette of Belgium respectively. Moon's paintings lack the botanical precision of Fitch, Miss Drake and others, but they have a dreamy quality, enhanced by the use of an air brush. The originals now belong to the American Orchid Society, having been sold by Sander and Sons during World War II.

LATER VICTORIAN ORCHID PAINTERS

Flower painting was a popular pastime in Victorian England and a number of paintings by amateur artists have survived to the present day. Notable among these is the work of John Day, an amateur orchid grower who lived at Tottenham in north London. Day painted orchids in his own fine collection, at Kew and at all the leading nurseries in London. Between the 1860s and 1886, he completed more than 2,300 watercolours, preserved in 53 volumes at Kew.

Nowadays the desire to record orchids that are flowering in a private collection can be satisfied by using a camera; in Victorian times the only way was to employ an artist. From 1879 until 1898, the Marquis of Lothian, who had the finest private orchid collection in Scotland, at Newbattle Abbey near Edinburgh, commissioned Florence Woolward to paint his finest specimens in full flower. These paintings, more than 300 in all, remain in the hands of the marquis's family and have yet to be seen in their full glory by the public. Fortunately, the marquis also commissioned Miss Woolward to prepare 80 plates and the text for the book *The Genus Masdevallia*, published in 1896, which remains an important and beautiful reference book for the genus.

At about the same time, in Paris, Emile Libreck was also amassing a fine collection of orchids, a display of

This beautiful, accurate lithograph of Dendrobium devonianum *by W. H. Fitch was one of hundreds he did for* Curtis's Botanical Magazine.

which won him the coveted Bronze Medal of the Société Nationale d'Horticulture de France. No doubt the same desire that drove the marquis to preserve the ephemeral beauty of his beloved orchids also inspired Libreck to commission Alexandre Brun to paint his collection. In many ways the paintings of Alexandre Brun have the same aura as those of Henry Moon, lacking the detail that botanists desire, but accurately demonstrating the overall appearance of the orchids.

ORCHID SOCIETIES AND PUBLICATIONS

The names and addresses of some orchid societies and their publications are given below.

AUSTRALIA
Australian Orchid Council Inc
Secretary: Mr D.J. Harris
36 East Ave, Black Forest
South Australia 5035

Publication: *Orchids Australia*

BELGIUM
Belgische Orchideeën Vereeniging
Mercatorstraat 50, 2018, Antwerp

De Orchideevriend Belgie
Bronstraat 21, 9700 Oudenaarde

Joint Publication: *Orchideeën*

Les Orchidophiles Réunis de BelgiQue
Daniel Deltenre, Rue de Bomeree 42
6110 Montignies-le-Tilleul

BERMUDA
Bermuda Orchid Society
Robert Mercer
P O Box HM19, Hamilton 5

BRAZIL
Nucleo Orquidofilos de Casa Branca
Professor Ary Marcondes Do Amaral,
av Francisco Nogueira/de Lima 722
"Desterro" 13.700
Casa Branca (SP)

DENMARK
Danish Orchid Society
Anders Nielsen, Vestervang 8330, Beder

Orchid Club of Denmark
Jorgen Listov-Saabye
Solsikkevej 7, DK-4600 Koge

ECUADOR
Asociacion Ecuatoriana de Orquidelogia
Max Konanz, Apartado 1033, Guayaquil

FRANCE
Société Française d'Orchidophile
Dr Maurice Grinfeder
8 rue des Saussaies, 75008 Paris

Publication: *L'Orchidophile*

GERMANY
Deutsche Orchideen-Gesellschaft EV
Herbert Degner, Weidenstrasse 7
4030 Ratingen

Publication: *Die Orchidee*

HAWAII
Honolulu Orchid Society Inc
Wilson Lee
1710 Pali Highway, Honolulu HI 96813

Pacific Orchid Society of Hawaii
Clarence Kelly
47-603 Hui Ulili Street, Kanoehe HI 96744

Joint publication: *Hawaii Orchid Journal*

HOLLAND
Nederlandse Orchideeën Vereeniging
Dr Ir H.G. Kronenberg
Hollandseweg 362, 6705 BD Wageningen

Publication: *Orchideeën* (jointly with
Belgian societies)

INDIA
Orchid Club of Bombay
P.K. Navatin
Sir Vithaldas Chambers
2nd Floor, 16 Appolo St, Bombay-1

The Orchid Society of India
Secretary, Botany Department
Punjab University, Chandigarh 160 014

Publication: *Journal of the Orchid Society
of India*

ITALY
Societa Italiana Orchidee
Mario dalla Rosa
26 via Bazzani, 00128 Rome

JAMAICA
Jamaica Orchid Society
Dr S.I. Terry
38 Hope Boulevard, Kingston 6

JAPAN
All Japan Orchid Society
Dr Toshinori Tanaka
3311-158-10-5, Jichi Medical School,
Minamikawachi-Machi, Kawachi-Gun,
Tochigi-Ken

KENYA
Kenya Orchid Society
M.H. Vincent, Box 24744, Nairobi

MEXICO
Asociacion Mexicana de Orquidelogia AC
Eric Hagsater
Cerrand de Moctezuma 16
La Herradur, 53920 Huizquilucan, Edo

Publication: *Orquidea*

NEW ZEALAND
Orchid Council of New Zealand
R.A. Clareburt,18 Littlejohn Street
Hillsborough 4, Auckland

New Zealand Orchid Society Inc
Ross Rucker, 51 King Edward Avenue
Bayswater, Auckland

Joint publication: *Orchids in New Zealand*

PAPUA NEW GUINEA
Orchid Society of Papua New Guinea
C.W. Webster, P O Box 2239
Boroko NCD

Publication: *Orchid Society of Papua New
Guinea News*

PHILIPPINES
Philippine Horticultural Society
Dr Vincente Saplala
c/o Green & Grow Inc, P O Box 125
College, Laguna

Philippine Orchid Society
Dr Victor Potenciano
c/o The Polymedic General Hospital Inc
163 E Delor Santos, Dandaluyong
Metro-Manila

SINGAPORE
The Orchid Society of South East Asia
Phoon Yoong Seng
22 Tosca Street, Singapore 1545

Publication: *The Malayan Orchid Review*

SOUTH AFRICA
Transvaal Orchid Society
Tessa A. Rakow
P O Box 5757, Johannesburg 2000

Publication: *South African Orchid Journal*

SPAIN
Club Amigo de las Orquideas
Peter Bourguignon
c/o Montearagon 8, 28033 Madrid

SWEDEN
Swedish Orchid Society
Dr Jan-Olof Jeppsson
Artholmsvagen 198, S-216 20 Malmo

SWITZERLAND
Schweizerische Orchideen-Gesellschaft
Erika Rusterholz
Bachserstrase 2, 8175 Neerach

Publication: *Die Orchidee* (jointly with
Deutsche Orchideen-Gesellschaft)

THAILAND
Orchid Society of Thailand
Professor Rapee Sagarik
6 Soi 41, Paholyothin Road, Bangkok 9

UNITED KINGDOM
Orchid Society of Great Britain
Dr Gary Firta
9 Harlands Close, Haywards Heath
West Sussex RH16 1PS

Publication: *Journal of The Orchid Society
of Great Britain*

Royal Horticultural Society
Orchid Section
80 Vincent Square, London SW1P 2PE

Publication: *The Orchid Review*

Scottish Orchid Society
Dorothea Macdonald
27 Dumgoyne Drive, Bearsden
Glasgow G61 3AP

UNITED STATES OF AMERICA
American Orchid Society Inc
6000 South Olive Avenue
West Palm Beach, Florida 33405

Publication: *Bulletin of the American Orchid Society*

VENEZUELA
Orchid Club de Venezuela
Neety ten Kortenaar
Apartado 89739, Caracas 1083-A

WEST INDIES
Barbados Orchid Circle
Dr Stephen Collins
5 Frere Pilgrim, Christ Church
Barbados

ZIMBABWE
Zimbabwe Orchid Society
R Weston
17 Nigils Lane, Borrowdale
P.O. Chisipite

OTHER PUBLICATIONS

Australian Orchid Review
14 McGill Street, Lewisham NSW 2049
AUSTRALIA

Orchid Digest: the Orchid Magazine of Western America
Secretary: Mrs Donald C. Dirks
1429 Graffigna Ave
Lodi, California 95240, USA

The search for orchids was never more dangerous than that for the wonderful Dendrobium phalaenopsis *var.* schroderianum *in New Guinea. The collector discovered it growing "among a great number of human skulls and bones" on ground where a cannibal tribe laid out their dead. Hostile and fearful of the spirits of their ancestors, the tribesmen were reluctant to collect the orchids, but tempted by "gorgeous handkerchiefs, beads, looking-glasses and brass wire...they boldly went and rooted out every plant." One of their idols, the god with golden eyes, was placed in the case with the orchids to take care of them on the journey back to London.*

INDEX OF COLOUR PLATES

ACKNOWLEDGEMENTS

b=bottom c=centre t=top l=left r=right

Cribb, Phillip *p152*
Private collection *pp6-9*

The portrait of Sir Joseph Banks on page 144 is a detail taken from an engraving (after the painting by Sir Thomas Lawrence) in the possession of the Royal Botanic Gardens, Kew. The illustration on page 153 is taken from the *Herbal* (1581) by Matthias de Lobel, and all other illustrations from nineteenth-century books and journals, in the Library at Kew. Illustrations frequently appeared more than once: in differerent issues of the same publication and in other publications; an economical use of laboriously hand-engraved plates.

Curtis's Botanical Magazine (1849) Plate 4429 *p155*
Day, John *Sketchbooks* 42-44 *p154t*
De Puydt, E. *Les Orchidées* (1880) *ppl30, 139, 145bl, 160*
The Gardeners' Chronicle (1882-1899) *ppl29, 132t, 133, 134t, 137t, 138b, 143, 146, 148, 151*
Linden, Lucien *Les Orchidées exotiques* (1894) *ppl35, 137b, 138t, 147, 150tl*
Lindley, John *Sertum Orchidacearum* (1838-42) *p54b*
Lindley, John *The Veqetable Kingdom* 3rd Edition (1853) *pl40b*
Revue horticulture Belge (1889) *ppl45br, 150tr*
Veitch, James *A Manual of Orchidaceaous Plants* (1894) *ppl32b, 140t, 141, 142t*
Watson, W. and Bean, W. *Orchids: Their Culture and Management* (1890) *ppl34b, 138c, 142t*
Woolward, Florence/The Marquis of Lothian *The Genus Masdevallia* (1891-96) *pl59*

Alexandre Brun's paintings were photographed by Graham Bush

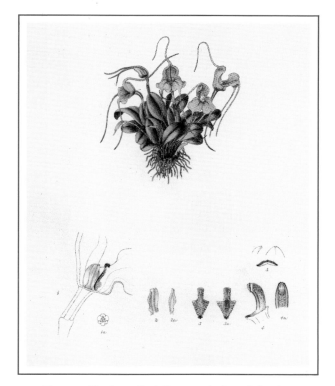

Florence Woolward's delicate painting of the tiny Masdevallia wageneriana, its flowers only $^3/_4$ in/19 mm across on stems 2 in/5 cm long, was made for The Genus Masdevallia.

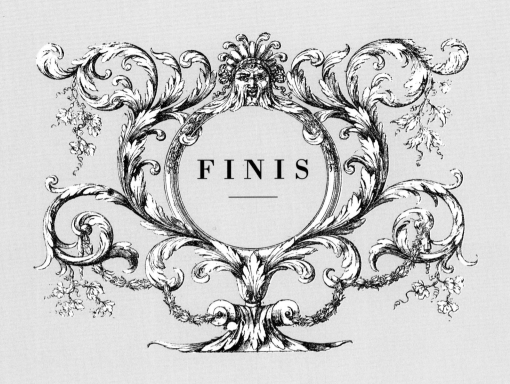

FINIS